THE MAGICK OF ASTAROTH

THE MAGICK OF
ASTAROTH

DAVID THOMPSON

TRANS MUNDANE
PUBLISHING
OCCULT KNOWLEDGE

To Lilith - who is patiently waiting for her own book.

"It's not worth doing something unless you're doing something that someone, somewhere, would much rather you weren't doing." - Terry Pratchett

Disclaimer:

None of the material in this book is intended to act as medical, financial, emotional, or lifestyle advice. No material, rituals or suggestions in this book replaces the advice of real medical professionals. The techniques and methods in this book can be used for the treatment of any medical conditions, whether physical, psychological, or emotional, direct or indirect or through implication. The material in this book is not intended to replace the advice of professionals. It is only intended to share spiritual information that is speculative in nature. If you choose to use this material, the author cannot accept any responsibility for the misuse of this information. This material can effect powerful change, use it responsibly.

All sigils in this book are original and copyrighted by David Thompson.

Table of Contents

1

Introduction

In this book, I plan to take a reader from perhaps being a neophyte magician, giving them the knowledge to form an understanding of magick, to a successful magician.

Knowledge which will help you become more knowledgeable about magick itself, and how and why we use spirits in magick, versus simply projecting energy into our reality.

In my previous books on Grecian Magick, I would focus on a single deity. In my High Magick Books, I usually listed multiple spirits in a single book. In this book, I will focus on one spirit, a fascinating spirit known as "Astaroth".

The more recent grimoires, such as Ars Goetia and Pseudomonarchia Daemonum, refer to Astaroth as a male spirit. After contact, I saw these books were incorrect, and that Astaroth was very much a feminine spirit. I contacted Astaroth during the writing of my book on Daemons and the Law of Attraction. Since then, I have worked with her many, many times.

In this book, we'll examine the magick one can work with

Astaroth, focusing on the areas of wealth and power.

There will be simple rituals to assist in a fast income boost, and more complex sequences designed to establish and maintain a strong income stream, be it working for yourself or starting your own business.

Interested in attaining a position of power? We'll look at Astaroth's abilities to help guide us to be in the right place at the right time, and directing us to meet people we can use to assist us in gaining power, be that power political, corporate, or physical power.

Astaroth will assist the magician using this system to achieve power. Achieve wealth.

Astaroth will be presented in both her forms: Daemoness and Goddess. Each aspect has unique energy when she arrives. In both forms, her energy is soft, loving, and welcoming. As a daemon, there are notes of a sharper energy, ready to help you if others need to be pushed out of your way. As a goddess, her energy is softer and carries an energy more like that of Aphrodite.

You can compare her to another Daemoness/Goddess; Lilith.

This book will also have examples of worksheets to assist you in defining your desires, and how to word these desires into effective statements, petitions, and sigils. I will have a link at the end of the book to a package to download with the worksheets and the sigils.

2

I was asked to write this book by Astaroth.

You see, I am "gifted". I can communicate with spirits, and occasionally see the future or aspects of the past. I say "gifted" because many people consider these types of psychic abilities "gifts". That's because someone, somewhere, decided to use the term "gifted" when it comes to psychic abilities. I'd like to find this person and set them down at my kitchen table and explain to them how disturbing such "gifts" can be, possibly using edged weapons and major league baseball bats. I know I have thrown astral bricks at my guides on occasions when these gifts raise their collective ugly heads. I need peace. I relish the quiet. The spirits will often provide me with none of that. They wish to be heard. This goes double if the spirit is an elder god or goddess, who wishes to be heard over all the mumbling of the followers of the main-stream deities.

But having these gifts has led me to where I am now. Why I am writing at this stage in my life?

I wanted an income stream independent of daily "work". For me, writing isn't really work. You see, I grew weary of pushing my reading services and trying to market monthly classes on magick, or trying to break into movies during a time when even the most talented people are being ignored by the gate-keepers in Hollywood.

So, I started writing these books. I am also gifted with the ability to write, stringing words together in specific orders to communicate information. And it's easy for me to write. I've written since I was in elementary school. I worked as a sports columnist right after high school and sold several short stories while in college. Writing books about magick just seemed like the thing to do right.

It combines my so-called "gift" of mediumship with my flair for the written word. I can channel (for lack of a better term) the deities I am writing about. They may not take over and guide my fingers while typing, but they are sending me streams of information.

Imagine being able to suddenly receive ten TV channels all at the same time. A bit confusing. I have to sift through the information and make sense out of it. Sometimes it's literal dictation. They speak and I write what they say, or I get images and emotions and I have to describe that in my words. Why some spirits can only send me images and others can talk to me has nothing to do with how powerful of a spirit they are. It depends on the energy flows around me at any one time. I happen to unconsciously block all the energy aimed at me. It's a learned technique after years of always hearing thoughts and voices. It was needed if I was to even attempt to live a normal life. I used to hear kids talking about me, only it was them thinking about me, never voicing their thoughts. So, I learned to block almost all energy sent towards me.

Another side effect of channeling is a surge of energy. No reason for caffeine, cocaine, or meth when channeling a spirit jolts my system such that I can't even sleep for days. For my sanity, I have to limit spirit contact.

Which brings up why spirits will get my attention in interesting ways and catch me off-guard. I have had spirits throw things at me, books or pens flying off my desk, being touched when I am half-asleep, waking me up at night with taps on my door, and sending messages via "gifted" friends of mine.

I got interrupted during the writing of my Daemons and Law of Attraction book a few months ago. I kept hearing my name being called by a woman's voice. This was followed by a floral scent, like vanilla blossoms. I wondered briefly where that was coming from and dismissed it as most likely my granny was visiting.

Then I was touched on my arm, followed by a scent of lilac.

Okay. You had my annoyance, but now you have my attention.

That *certainly* wasn't my granny, who usually sends a floral scent. So, and with great hesitation, I quieted my mind, dropped into an altered mental state, and Astaroth walked into my life.

This was how Fortuna got my attention. It was how Apollo made himself known to me.

After writing a brief chapter about Astaroth, she reached out (literally) and asked me to write a book about her.

You may not believe what you will read next about Astaroth. So many in the community will scoff, some might even shout, and more than a few will direct invectives at me.

But, Astaroth is a Goddess.

After hundreds of years of mistranslations and mistakes,

Astaroth wants her story told.

And here it is.

3

Who is Astaroth? A Daemon or a Goddess?

According to the Ars Goetia, Astaroth is the 29th spirit, mighty and a great duke.

At some point in the Middle Ages, Astaroth suddenly switched genders, and the feminine aspect of this goddess was lost. Two modern occult writers, Lon Milo DuQuette and Christopher Hyatt, have put forward the idea that Astaroth is "a thinly disguised version of the goddess Astarte...."

As Astarte, her lineage can be traced further back to Canaan and Phonetician cultures, as a fertility, sex, love, and (bizarrely enough) war goddess.

To my mind, this brings Astaroth into focus as a quite powerful goddess in her own right, and not as the traditional daemon, who is often described as a nude man with dragon hands, feet, and wings

Some authors think the confusion which led to her being considered male occurred when the Hebrew bible was being translated into Greek and Latin, and the translators confused the gender with the plural forms of her names.

I can't really speak to that, but I can only go by my own experiences.

I first encountered Astaroth during research into daemons for one of my fantasy books. That's when I reached out to Astaroth. I felt a very definite feminine energy in my temple space. Her energy was a lot like Aphrodite, with the force of Lilith. I was concerned, because I was going only by what I'd researched in the Solomon Seals, or the Ars Goetia, and I wasn't expecting a feminine energy. This led me to research her a lot more, and I delved into her background.

That was when I'd read material by DuQuette and Hyatt, which made the observation that Astaroth was a form of the Canaanite goddess, Astarte. It was after reading a book on Lilith, and how the early monothesitic religions turned her into a daemon, I realized why I'd gotten a feminine energy: Astaroth was an aspect of Astarte, and Astarte was an earlier name for Aphrodite.

In this book, I'll cover working with her when she manifests in her form as a Daemon, and when she'll manifest in her form as a goddess. She has a dual nature, and we'll be summoning her in both her forms. In one form, the Daemon, she will project a great deal of power, which is helpful when wanting to manifest personal power and strength. As a Goddess, her energy is softer, nurturing and perfect for the energy of wealth, abundance when it concerns families, also with attracting romance, and as a personal Patron Goddess.

What I present in the way of rituals is just scratching the surface of this complex Goddess. I mean, the rituals in this book to be a starting point for your own explorations of magick with

Astaroth.

Use my words as a jumping off point.

4

Channeling Astaroth

What follows is what she gave to me to explain her origins, the world at that time, the old gods and goddesses, and how she became to be Astaroth, and my attempts to communicate that with you.

But first, a brief concept you may not be familiar with: Spiritual parents and child spirits.

Yes, you read that right, spirits can create energy and form new spirits. Like with humans (and the other creatures), it takes two to create a third. The Law of Attraction functions in this manner. A single thought can lead to another, similar thought, which then creates a third thought.

Spirits are thought forms. You. Me. The cashier at Taco Bell. All of us are thought forms. And all of us are connected.

Humans are the vessel in which our souls inhabit. Our souls were created by other souls. And we ALL were created by a creator soul, making us children of the creator.

No… Stop right there. The creator isn't Jehovah. Nope, not Yahweh. If you can't grasp that, I suggest you return this book to where you bought it.

According to ancient myths (myths no less valid than the Abrahamic religions, the Grecian religions, the Hindu religions), Astaroth is more directly our creator than those other elder gods. She can be linked to the goddess Asherah, a consort of the ancient Ugarit god El, with whom she gave birth to multiple deities, one of which is the god we know now as Yahweh. This makes her more of our "creator" than any other gods or goddesses.

I was tasked with looking beyond our current prehistory, during a period between the major cataclysmic events of asteroid impacts, comet impacts, which destroyed four previous civilizations, to see where all these elder gods originated.

Astaroth asked me to consider the following: We are now in the fifth human civilization. We also have had many gods and goddesses for the last 250,000 years. But they're not really gods. They're actually highly advanced human spirits.

During the third civilization, some humans achieved a level of evolution that allowed them to become immortal while in a physical body. They could separate from those bodies and still interact with everyone else. What the New Age folks now call "ascension". It's nothing new.

After that civilization went "kaboom", about twenty immortals stayed around to help reestablish human civilization. And along came the civilization called "Atlantis".

And those immortals were joined by a few more, and they assisted again.

In fact, many of the guide spirits are literally higher-level beings who "fell" in order to incarnate on the earth as humans, and assist humans. So, there's quite a few hanging around.

In fact, the pyramids are from one of those past civilizations. Many megalithic structures are from previous civilizations. Göbekli Tepe in south-east Turkey is another clue to the past civilizations. Researchers are finally piecing it together.

I have written about this in my Aphrodite, Hermes, and Apollo books. This is the origin of most of the gods humans have worshiped. I'm not sure where Yahweh comes into this. He's more like a easily angered dude that is a weird uncle who just shows up one day, wanting to sleep on the couch and not leaving. Then claiming he owns the house, and everyone else has to pack up and leave.

Astaroth became a "daemon" only because the men in charge of the religions made her into a daemon. The same with Lilith.

Any strong feminine divine was a threat to their control of the planet. So, these goddesses had to become daemons. The tribal leaders and heads of religious sects worked very hard to spread stories about beings like Lilith and Astaroth, scaring people away from calling upon or praying to these goddesses.

5

Your Desire

Although many people will work a ritual to Astaroth with no preparation, it's always best to clearly define your desire before writing a petition or crafting a sigil.

In the book "Eric", fantasy author Terry Pratchett summed it up like this:

"The whole point of the wish business was to see to it that what the client got was exactly what he asked for and exactly what he didn't really want."

I have lost count of how many people I know who have successfully manifested something in very unexpected ways. It's not always a pleasant surprise.

For example, my father attempted to use common manifestation methods to manifest a new truck.

He knew this woman who claimed to be some guru or something, and she told him how to manifest. She left a lot out of the instructions.

My father got his new truck alright.

He was driving his old one when traffic began to back up. As he passed a car on his right, another car attempted to pull into traffic and, in the words we use a lot in Texas, "T-boned the snot out of my dad's truck."

Ambulances were called because my old man was injured. And yeah, after the litigation dust settled, he limped out of it all with a new truck. But, some twenty years later, that back injury has him in a walker after multiple surgeries. Not the best way to have your desire manifest.

So, we have to define what we desire correctly. It might have helped my old man if he'd said "Bring me a new truck in a safe manner," or even "Bring me the opportunity to buy a new truck," or some such phrasing. But he never thought about asking a being. He might have prayed to his deity, but that particular thought form really needs direction to have things work out well.

Therefore, most books on magick have sections about helping you define what you want. The biggest key to successful magick is not thinking that you'll manifest your desire, but *knowing* you'll manifest your desire.

Which explains why many (most) have trouble manifesting anything big.

This is where Daemonic magick comes in. As long as you trust someone like Astaroth to bring you your desire safely, she will absolutely bring you the desire. After working a ritual, get ready to receive, because she will deliver. (See the chapter on Wealth for an *Opening To Receive* ritual)

So, what's a good way to figure out what you really, really want?

Start with what you DON'T want.

We've all seen this in action. "I know what I don't want now!"

you might say after ordering tacos de sesos and finding out it's actually goat brains with chunks of onion. So, you'd be better off ordering *"Carne asada"* or *"Carne molida"* then add *"con todo"*. Which is grilled steak or ground beef tacos with everything.

The final chapter in this book reveals some worksheets designed to assist you in narrowing down your desire and working out the statements needed for each ritual. Use the worksheets to also create any Chaos sigils you wish to create, which will combine the energy of Astaroth with your desire. Of course, these worksheets are available as a download on my website:

https://davepsychic.com/astaroth-downloads/

The worksheets and Astaroth sigil are in Adobe Acrobat format, and you will need the Adobe Acrobat Reader to open and view these. They are designed to be printed on standard letter-sized paper.

The magick begins to work as you begin to define what it is you want, and in what shape or form is best for you. So, the longer you spend on defining your desire, the longer the magick has to build up. It builds pressure while you write out your desire. This pressure builds, and when you work the ritual, the pressure will send the desire out into our reality.

You also need to handwrite the desire. Just as you hand write the petition; handwriting is very important in this step. In my experiences, jotting the ideas down by hand, using pencil or pen, on scraps of paper, seems to make the concepts stick. I know in college, my handwritten notes (although illegible for the most part) caused the lecture to stick in my memory. Magick is the same way: magick depends on sinking into your subconscious and causing events to manifest.

So, write your ideas for your desire down by hand.

Crafting your Petition

When writing your petition to Astaroth, look at ways to phrase your request so that Astaroth can bring you this desire and in a timely manner. Try to be as specific as possible. Astaroth and magick will look for the easiest ways to bring your desire to you. If you want more money, but you ONLY say "Bring me more money", Astaroth might take a look at the situation and then your boss asks you to work multiple overtime shifts. The desire is granted: More money. BUT you may have wanted a small lottery win instead.

As always, phrase your request as if you are asking someone for a special favor. Use "please" and "thank you", as that is only polite.

Then write out the petition by hand. In the past, I have typed out the petition, but once in ritual, Apollo suggested I write the petition by hand. This was interesting because, one, I had not summoned Apollo, and two, the suggestion resonated. My experience now seems to prove out the effectiveness of handwriting a petition, versus typing it out and then sending it to the printer. I still outline the ritual steps by typing, because it's often difficult to recall each line of a summoning, unless it's a ritual or being I've summoned many times before.

Preparation for your ritual.

Aside from defining your desire and writing out your petition, you also need to mentally prepare for the ritual. It doesn't matter if you are working the full ritual or a simplistic pathworking ritual. Preparation is key.

I will either walk through the woods here, being lucky enough to live on 40 acres of pine forest on the side of a big hill (or small mountain) in New England. The solitude and silence allow me to center, dissolve away the stress of daily life, and decompress.

I call this my "pre-ritual cooling down". I also do this when preparing for a reading.

For pathworking, I will often take a seat in the woods on an old stump, and meditate in nature, then work the mental ritual there.

I recognize few of my readers may have access to such a piece of land, but even when I was in Los Angeles, I still managed to find small, secluded parts of parks to sit and center myself. Find a quiet corner somewhere and sit, and just exist.

Even if that spot is a bathroom.

I don't expect people to spend hours in meditation preparing for a ritual, but try to carve out at least 15 minutes of "me time" before going into ritual. It'll shift the magick and allow it to work easier.

6

Astaroth's Sigils

Astaroth has an established sigil, usually found when anyone searches the internet's cosmic school of mystery.

And now, I present another sigil for her, one to be used while working the daemonic rituals in this book. This sigil is a bit complex, but you will use it printed. If you wish, you can trace it out and put it on a daemonic candle for Astaroth. (This isn't the same as the new sigil I drew for her in my Law of Attraction book). She later showed me two master sigils to be used with the rituals in this book: A Master Power Sigil and a Master Wealth Sigil.

For Astaroth, as a goddess, I have created a simple sigil, easy to copy by hand. It is like the other sigils created for the Grecian deities in my other books. This sigil can be drawn onto candles or incorporated into other artwork for your altar to Astaroth.

Activating these sigils.

After copying or printing the sigils, full size found in the downloads, and at the back of the book, you activate them either one at a time or all at once, while in your magick space. You summon Astaroth, either with her Goddess Ritual, or her ENN in a Daemonic ritual.

Astaroth's Daemonic Sigil

Astaroth

Astaroth's Goddess Sigil

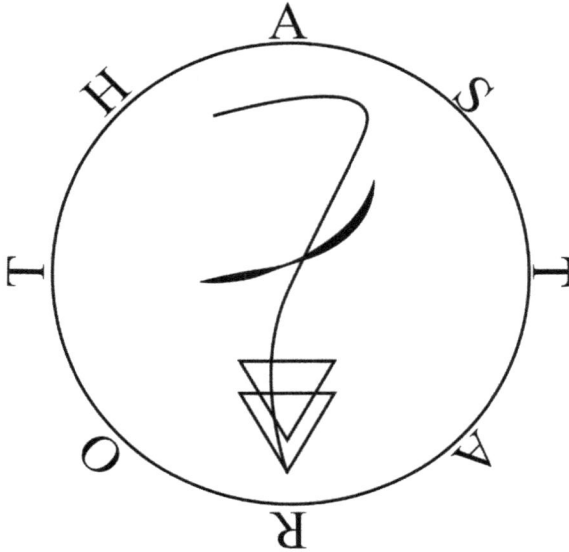

Master Sigils

Astaroth interrupted me one evening when I wanted to switch everything off and go to bed. I was looking at how little I had left to write and figured I was done for the evening. Time to head to bed, right?

But no, she tickled me on my neck. I thought a bug had landed, or something else. Then it happened again. I vaguely saw her then, leaning against the office door. I could swear she had an arched eyebrow, and possibly smoking a "Marlborough". Like a bad-ass chick who's waiting impatiently for my attention.

Seems I wasn't quite as finished as I'd thought.

She told me I had to draw up some more sigils for her. I saw the design for a Master Power Sigil, and Master Wealth Drawing

Sigil. And I had to get these drawn out "before you forget."

So, here they are!

Activating these sigils is easy. Work a ritual to Astaroth in her daemon form. Have her activate them both. Print out on regular paper, and make several copies. Keep them with you, under your bed, in a wallet/purse.

You can also ask an artist to create a metal talisman of them. I highly recommend a good friend, who has a page on FaceBook, the Talimancer. See the links in the appendix.

Master Power Sigil

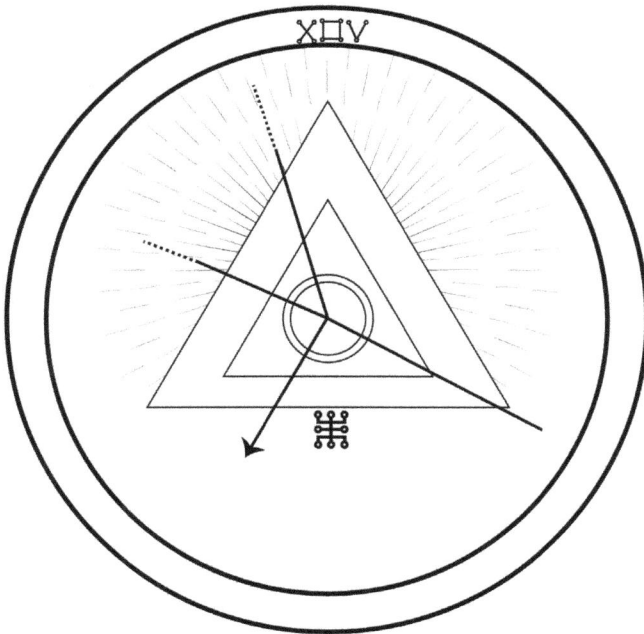

Master Wealth Draw Sigil

7

Sigils as Talismans

A sigil can be turned into a talisman. Using the sigil worksheets, you can turn your petition into a sigil. Before doing this, you need to rewrite your desire into a single sentence. Since you will convert this into a series of letters, it is best to limit the words in a sigil desire.

When it comes to sigils, the statement needs to be worded as a present-tense or past-tense desire. Do not write it as a future event, but write it as IF it has already happened.

A good example of a sigil statement is: "My book is a best seller on Amazon." Or "I receive over twenty thousand dollars a month."

There's a long-winded explanation of why this is needed. It's how this sigil magick works. Please don't argue and just follow the directions. Don't worry HOW the desire will come to you. Let Astaroth bother with that.

In your statement, add Astaroth, so you are adding her energy to your sigil!

Say "Astaroth helped make my book a best seller" or

"Astaroth brought me over ten well-paying clients."

Also note: spell out all numbers. Specify what TYPE of currency you use for money. I asked Lucifer for several thousand for a project. Lucifer has a sense of humor and loves a good lesson. I found an old, dusty wallet on the sidewalk, no ID. Inside was... $10,000. It was just in currency from a Central American country where it was worth, maybe, ten dollars.

So, the lesson is, specify currency. Such as Ten Thousand Dollars (US, Canada, Australia), Euros, Pounds, Pesos, etc.

Once you have a sigil, it's okay to keep working on it. Play with arranging the letters into artistic shapes. I like to use a "C" or "G" to encircle most of the rest of the design. Combine M with N, T with an H. W can be both a W and a V. Have fun.

Once you have a sigil, you go into ritual and ask Astaroth to energize and activate your sigil.

A Talisman is a sigil that is turned into a piece of jewelry. You can hire an artist to etch it into a small medallion, and carry it as a key chain, or wear as a necklace. I have several of my sigils as beautiful talismans.

8

Rituals to Astaroth

Before we go into the process of manifesting power and wealth, I'll cover the two basic rituals that can be worked for Astaroth. A standard High Magick ritual in her form as a Daemon, and a standard ritual to her in her form as a Goddess.

You won't need a sizable space for these rituals. Unless you want to move furniture and draw out an enormous pentagram on the floor, complete with copies of Astaroth's sigils on all four cardinal directions, plus five or more white candles on each point of the pentagram, one just needs a small space to work with Astaroth.

Personally, I had to use a TV tray table and only set up in my bedroom when needing to work a ritual for a long time. So, any space will work, and you don't have to walk around your space defining the circle unless you really feel you have to do this. If you do set up and work in an area frequented by others, I strongly suggest you work the Banishing of the Pentagram each time prior to working a ritual to anyone. I have this ritual in the appendix, as well as part of the material you can download. If you are using a private space, then performing the Banishing of the Pentagram is usually only needed every few weeks or months.

Reserve any candles used for her and don't use them for any other ritual.

In these rituals, I instruct you to meditate and drop into a light trance state. This is also known as "gnosis" or Alpha. It's a state of mind where you can daydream easily. It's a state of mind where you connect to your subconscious and can hear, or see, things normally filtered out by your conscious mind. It's the state of mind you might find yourself in when attending a boring meeting or lecture, and you begin to drift away from the surrounding situation, and your imagination opens up. This is the state I normally use when opening up to listen to spirit or do remote viewing.

Never, ever allow yourself to go into Alpha if you are driving or doing anything that requires your total attention.

Make sure you are comfortable in your altar space. There should be no interruptions, such as loud noises or cell phones, to distract you. Put the kids to bed, make sure the pets are settled down. Good luck if you live in a crowded urban area, as it's hard to control noises in a city. I know, I lived in Los Angeles. The best times for rituals there were between 2am and 3am. Even then, a helicopter could suddenly fly overhead.

Darkness. Sometimes this is preferred when working any ritual where you summon a daemonic spirit. When working with a goddess, pick a time of day where you feel the most comfortable. In classic Greece, many people would commune with the gods in temples where the light was kept low. It was usually smoky in these temples, filled with incense and wood fires. (I bet their robes reeked of smoky and funky incense when they left the temple.)

In writing your petition, use phrases such as "please bring me" and "I thank you" as it's only polite. None of these rituals will attempt to bind or force Astaroth. I feel strongly that we, as magicians, should never attempt to force or threaten any spirit. This also goes for the tradition of forcing a daemon into a "spirit house". Restraining a daemon to a specific spot and using angels to guard against any daemon trying to possess you or "escaping" and doing harm. If you feel that you have summoned a dark entity, a true evil being, you definitely did not summon Astaroth in any of her forms. Even as a daemon, Astaroth will bring soothing energy, like the energy of one's mother, not a wicked evil daemon from the depths of the Underworld.

With that said, let's take a look at a couple of "standard" rituals I use for working with Astaroth.

(Please note: You do not have to summon Astaroth when you only have a petition. Also ask her to drop by just to talk, or to feel her energy. Get to know her before asking for large desires.)

9

Standard Ritual of Astaroth the Daemon

For this ritual, you will need an altar space, and the following items:

Candles. Basic altar candles can be any color. I prefer white and black. Use a red candle for Astaroth in her daemonic aspect. It's totally optional to draw her sigil on this red candle. If so, use silver, as that looks really cool.

- o Incense and Incense burner.
- o Specific candle for the purpose of the ritual.
- o Offering bowl.
- o Offering
- o Fireproof bowl, as you will burn the petition.
- o Optional items: Crystals, alternatives to incense such as essential oils, and alternatives to candles such as LED candles. I also have vials of oils made up for rituals, such as a money-draw oil, a crown of success oil, and others as needed.

Offerings

This is where Astaroth as a daemon differs from her aspect as a goddess - the offering.

Traditional daemonic offerings are encouraged in this type of ritual: anything that represents life, such as a raw egg, piece of red meat, or your own blood.

When using a blood offering (sacrifice) you will need a diabetic lancet and her sigil printed on paper. This will act as her Daemonic offering. When it comes time to give her the offering, prick your finger (doesn't matter which finger) and place a single drop of blood on her printed sigil. Then, hold up the paper and say the offering statement, then burn the paper, dropping the paper into a fireproof bowl. I use two aluminum pie plates to hold paper when I burn it. I then stir the burning paper to make sure it completely burns.

There really is no alternative to giving an offering. Try to stick with what is written above.

Incense

Incense for Astaroth as a Daemon needs to be a traditional resin blend, using Dragon's Blood. I have a blend I made with frankincense, white copal, and Dragon's Blood. It has a unique aroma and produces a lot of smoke. During a ritual to Astaroth, I have had the incense smoke begin to swirl, sending off streamers of smoke, and often I can see her face in the incense smoke.

If you choose to burn a stick or cone, go with a high-quality brand, in frankincense or Dragon's Blood.

Candles

For the altar, I use both a white and black candle, with a single candle for Astaroth. As a daemon, use a red candle. You need to make sure this candle isn't used for any other ritual. You can draw on it Astaroth's sigil, but that isn't necessary.

Candles for the desire. For money, I always suggest you use gold. Gold is the universal color of wealth. For power, use red, as red is a color of power and energy. These candles should be small spell candles, and place these in a heavy candle holder, as you will need to burn these completely. After the ritual, you can move the candle to a safe spot, but always make sure you can burn the candle safely. I have used the bathtub, the oven, and a clean fireplace. A small spell candle burns quickly, which is why I recommend those.

If you cannot burn a candle, for whatever reason, go with a small battery powered fake candle. Paint it the colors you need, and on the spell candle, allow it to stay on until the battery dies.

The Ritual

This is simply an outline you can use to create your own rituals. It's a basic daemonic ritual, and a lot of the extras in a traditional ritual are left out, as they really serve no real purpose. Have everything you need next to you. If you forget the petition, for example, (like I do) you need to cast your circle again.

To work a standard ritual, here are the usual steps:

Light the incense and candles (except for the desire candle).

Lights off.

Cast your circle and work the Banishing of the Pentagram if it is needed.

Settle yourself in and relax.

Breathe deeply and allow yourself to go into a slight trance state.

Meditate for a moment on the goal of the ritual, and read over the petition you plan to use.

Now, summon Astaroth, saying her common ENN three times.

> *Tasa Alora foren Ashtaroth*
> *Tasa Alora foren Ashtaroth*
> *Tasa Alora foren Ashtaroth*
> *Astaroth, Daemon of Power*
> *Astaroth, Daemon of Wealth*
> *I ask that you join with me in my space*
> *Be with me! Commune with me!*
> *Astaroth, it is my deepest desire that —*
> > *Read your petition*
> *Astaroth, I ask that you bring to me that I have requested in this petition.*

(If burning an additional candle for this desire, take hold of it now)

Astaroth, I ask that you now bless this candle so that it will bring to me my desire.

(Light the candle and make sure it's in a safe location)

And in gratitude for your assistance and for being here to listen to my prayer,

I hereby give to you this humble _____ (the offering if it is **NOT** a blood offering)

If you are giving her a blood offering, say the following after thanking her for listening to your petition:

Astaroth, I now sacrifice my living essence to you,

In gratitude for acting on my petition.

Prick your finger (any finger) with the diabetic lancet and allow a single drop of blood to land on her sigil. Hold the sigil up and touch it to the flame of her candle, and say,

To you, I give over this essence, Astaroth.

As the sigil burns, drop it into the fireproof container and make sure it burns completely. Stir the ashes to make sure it's totally consumed. After the ritual, toss the ashes outside, allowing them to be spread with the wind.

Time to finish the ritual. Place the petition or sigil on the altar and hold your hands over it. Take a moment to visualize energy flowing into the petition or sigil.

Oh Astaroth, please charge this (sigil or petition) with your energy, mix your energy with mine and work to make this manifest - so it is written, so it is done.

I thank you for being here with me, Astaroth, and

you may now depart and please come again when I next call upon you!

That pretty much wraps up this ritual.

If offering something other than blood, allow this offering to stay on your altar, on her sigil, until the following day, then take it outside and place the offering into nature. If it's an offering of wine or spirit, pour the offering out onto the ground.

10

Standard Ritual Astaroth the Goddess

If you have read my books on Grecian goddesses, such as Aphrodite or Tyche, you will be familiar with this ritual. It uses the same basic structure as those other rituals and differs from the Daemonic rituals to Astaroth.

You'll need the following items:

- o Altar candles
- o Astaroth's dedicated Goddess Candle
- o Astaroth's Goddess Sigil
- o Incense. Either frankincense resin or a stick of honeysuckle or lilac.
- o Offering and offering bowl
- o Candle to represent your desire
- o Your Petition
- o Optional items: Crystals, Goblet of Water, Athame

Of the items above, you can make substitutions, such as essential oils for incense, and fake LED type candles for actual candles.

Offerings

As a goddess, do not go with what you'd offer to a daemon. Stick to either the most common offering from the ancient world; wine, or go with flowers, sweet breads, cake, heavy cream with honey, organic honey, or mead.

As with the other rituals, leave the offering on Astaroth's sigil overnight, then take the offering outside. Any alcoholic beverage used as an offering, pour onto the ground. All other offerings leave out for any animals in your area.

Incense Blends

As a goddess, Astaroth loves a good incense blend. If you are using resin on charcoal, mix up an incense blend using frankincense, amber, sandalwood, and benzoin. You can also purchase resin samplers and make a blend from those.

Otherwise, shop for an incense blend designed for a goddess such as Aphrodite or Inanna.

If you decide to use incense sticks, shop for a high-quality stick, in a floral fragrance, such as honeysuckle, lilac, or lavender.

If you need to use essential oils, make up a blend with lilac, rose and any floral oil.

Candles

I always try to be very clear when it comes to candles and

magick, as many times the ritual candle itself must be burned completely, and it's difficult to supervise a long burning candle, so it's very important to burn the candle in a safe spot. You can use the glass candles, known as five- or seven-day votive candles. For a ritual purpose, you can also use fake candles. If you can't find a green or gold fake candle, then use paint to color the fake candle the color it needs to be, and keep it on until the battery dies.

For Astaroth's candle, she prefers a pale candle, like pale pink or pale blue. In a pinch, go with white. For artificial candles, choose her color and simply switch it off when done.

The Ritual

Like the Daemonic ritual, this is a simple outline that you can use when creating your own rituals to Astaroth. In this one, Astaroth is called upon as a Canaanite goddess - which will sound familiar if you have ever worked my Grecian rituals to Aphrodite or Fortuna.

Gather up all materials needed. Have your petition written out, and the sigil if you have turned your desire into a sigil. Select a specific candle for this ritual.

When ready, light the incense and candles. If you are using charcoal and resin, make sure to get that charcoal puck going. It should be covered in white ash before starting the ritual.

Drop some incense onto the glowing charcoal, and cast your circle. If you are using a temporary altar space, be sure to work the Banishment as well, to eject any non-beneficial energy from your space.

Here are the basic steps in an easy-to-follow list:

Light incense and candles

Cast your circle

Sit and meditate for a moment.

Now call to Astaroth

Astaroth! Goddess of Life, Goddess of the Field, Goddess of the Hearth.

Astaroth, you who have been known by name names,

Astarte, Iananna, Venus, and others,

Join with me in my space, talk with me,

Grace me with your divine presence.

Astaroth! I call to you now in your form as a Loving Goddess.

Pause a moment - stretch out your awareness to see if she is near you now.

Astaroth, I now ask that -

(Read your petition)

Pause now, and visualize the outcome of your desire manifesting. Run a daydream where it all occurs for you in the way you wish for it to manifest. Take your time doing this. (Hint: This is actually the key to how it all works.)

If you are using a special candle, pick it up now and say:

Oh, Goddess Astaroth! Please bless this candle to

bring to me my desire!

Light the candle and set it into its holder.
Pick up your offering and now say:

Oh Astaroth, please accept this humble offering, in gratitude for listening to my petition.

Place the offering into the offering bowl, and place that on her sigil.

Now, time to charge the petition or sigil with energy. Hold your hands over the petition or sigil and say the following:

Intro this petition, I now direct great power, power from you, Astaroth, and my own inner power, to make this desire manifest. And so it is!

After a minute or two, the petition or sigil is charged.

Oh, Goddess Astaroth, our time now is done. I thank you for your presence in my circle.

You may depart peacefully now and please return when I next call upon you!

At this point, you can walk out of the circle.

Keep your sigil or petition near you for the next few days. You can place it under a pillow, or in a wallet or purse.

The next day, discard the offering outside.

11

Pathworking

Pathworking is a unique system of working with a spirit, which uses sensory visualizations to create an energy path to the astral and contact the intended spirit. It's also a form of initiation into some mystical traditions where the initiate works a path towards a spiritual goal, such as enlightenment.

I use this term for a way of quickly placing you into a lightly altered state of mind, which aligns your energy to that of the spirit, daemon, deity, or other being you are seeking communion with. It places you on a level plane with the desired being.

When working in this manner, practice several times going into a light "alpha" state, a dreamy state of mind where it's easy to daydream. This isn't daydream manifesting, and unlike a normal daydream, you need to maintain control over your thoughts while in this state.

That's sometimes harder that it appears.

I, for example, can drift off course while in alpha. My guide Daniel says it's a problem for me, and he also says I have the attention span of a gnat on speed.

(But that's just his opinion, and he's a petty — *OH LOOK! A squirrel!*)

So, practice going into alpha, use meditation audios if you need to. It's not cheating to go into alpha using an audio, even if some gurus scoff at the use of guided audios, it's a proven method and I suggest you try it.

I have gotten to the point where I can drop into that light trance state and continue to work and focus, but that's three decades of doing this, I don't expect a person who is new to this to master it quickly, but keep trying. That is the key - continue to try.

12

Pathworking Astaroth in her Daemonic form

In my book on Daemons and the Law of Attraction, I present a pathworking to Astaroth which is quick and easy to master.

I'll present it here and explain each detail:

- An open country garden.
- The smell of fresh flowers. Watch as a Honeysuckle blooms, and opens up.
- Bluebirds land on a branch above you. See its red breast and bright blue back.
- A warm, fresh breeze hits your face.

You begin by allowing yourself to go into alpha. Then visualize the garden. Maybe a bright sky overhead, a light breeze, and it's warm, like a sunny spring afternoon. Astaroth loves being in a garden, and this sets up an astral space which will allow her to appear and interact with you.

The next phase is psychically activating your sense of smell, which right now is purely imagination. But the key is this: as you imagine it happening, it will actually manifest in the astral. Honeysuckle is a fragrance that Astaroth loves and is one of her favorite offerings. Then you add the visual of the flower opening up, blooming, which signifies the opening up of the portal to allow Astaroth to be with you.

Astaroth then sends a bluebird. The bird will land and observe you for a moment. You should try your best to see the bird, how bright its blue feathers are, and the redness of the breast feathers. If you do not know what a typical North American bluebird looks like, do take a moment to look up photos of bluebirds.

The breeze will show that she has arrived, and you signal this by imagining the breeze hitting your face.

She'll materialize in your daydream. She may appear physically, projecting her preferred form to you, or you may just feel her presence.

*Do not worry if you can't detect her being near you. She'll be there. If you continue to have worries that she is not actually there, then ask her for signs she is around. Then be on alert for signs like birds, flowers or even aromas around you.

When pathworking, you do not need to give an offering. However, it's nice if you would set out a small glass of wine, or a fresh flower on her sigil.

Daemonic Pathworking Ritual

Here's the usual pathworking ritual I use for Astaroth.

> Go into a light trance.
>
> Visualize each step as outlined above.
>
> When the goddess appears, greet her by projecting

your words to her. You can also whisper if you wish, but mental projection works just as well.

Visualize your desire. Go into as much detail as you can, making it a mental movie.

What will it feel like when this desire manifests? Hold on to this emotion.

After a few moments with this visualization, ask Astaroth to assist you in making this manifest.

Be silent for a minute or two, then ask her if she has anything to tell you.

Send her a brief burst of pink light. Imagine this light going from the top of your head and into Astaroth's body. This is the loving light of gratitude.

Tell her goodbye, and any other positive phrases you wish to tell her.

Breathe a bit, then a cleansing breath. Open your eyes. The ritual is finished.

13

Pathworking Astaroth in her Goddess Form

I haven't included pathworking in any of my previous books on Grecian Goddesses, but it is certainly possible to work such a ritual to any deity no matter the pantheon. Pathworking is more closely associated with Daemons than other beings, but it's just as effective as most other rituals.

Pathworking is recommended only after you have run at least one ritual to Astaroth before doing the pathworking method.

The visuals for Astaroth in her Goddess form differ from the daemonic visuals. For some images, you may wish to do an image search of those areas to see what they might have looked like thousands of years ago. Using images from ancient Canaan and Mesopotamia will resonate with her goddess form, and draw to you the energy that was felt in temples from ancient times.

The visuals are as follows:

A hot day, with no clouds in the sky.

An oasis in the desert, surrounded by goats and camels.

A beautiful woman approaches you, her face covered

in a veil.

> The woman's eyes stare at you, then she blinks.
>
> You are now inside an ancient temple, tan rock walls.
>
> Smoke surrounds you.

At this point, Astaroth will appear to you.

   The work the ritual as you would when using the other visuals

Go into a light trance.

> Visualize each step as outlined above.
>
> When the goddess appears, greet her by projecting your words to her. You can also whisper if you wish, but mental projection works just as well.
>
> Visualize your desire. Go into as much detail as you can, making it a mental movie.
>
> What will it feel like when this desire manifests? Hold on to this emotion.
>
> After a few moments with this visualization, ask Astaroth to assist you in making this manifest.
>
> Be silent for a minute or two, then ask her if she has anything to tell you.
>
> Send her a brief burst of pink light. Imagine this pink light going from the top of your head and into Astaroth's body. This is the loving light of gratitude.
>
> Tell her goodbye, and any other positive phrases you wish to tell her.
>
> Breathe a bit, then a cleansing breath. Open your eyes. The ritual is finished.

14

Power Sequence

Before we get too deep into how Astaroth can assist you in gaining power, we must first define what you think of as "being powerful."

Is it physical? Being able to lift or perform feats of strength? For this, we'd look at methods of having Astaroth assist you in gaining physical strength. I would imagine this would need assistance in the form of trainers and coaches. Gaining strength is part magick and part physical. I doubt just the magick part would work sufficiently on its own to give you great strength.

But what is great strength to you?

Carrying in a lot of grocery bags? Lifting heavy bags of cement or gravel at a construction site?

Or do you want to achieve and amass political power? Power at your job?

Depending on which direction you want to go, there's a different aspect of Astaroth you will petition. You may also decide to enter into a pact (strongly suggested) to achieve this goal, as it's a long-term goal, not something that can happen in a few weeks.

Once you have defined which type of power you wish to manifest, you will then begin the Power Ritual Sequence. Certain rituals will need to be performed, in the order presented, to best set-up your new reality and to manifest your ultimate desire.

We start with protection. As you move forward, gaining power, you might make people jealous and that jealousy can lead to attacks, either energy attacks (projected jealousy) and verbal or printed attacks. I have been on the receiving end of both types of attacks, especially when I was a successful photographer. We'll use Astaroth as a daemon for this, as sometimes, a good defense is a good offensive attack.

Then Charm and Charisma. You've seen those people. Think of a popular persona, see how they can simply project this charm and people get all starry-eyed just looking at them. They can be downright weird people, but they still will charm you and cause you to be led to their side of the argument. This is a very powerful talent, and it's easily achieved using Astaroth in her Goddess form.

Next is Power Aura, and projecting that aura. This projection can work in person, on a stage, or even via the media. By projecting this, people will feel your power by just looking at you, in person or in a video, or still photograph. In this ritual, you can summon Astaroth in her daemon form.

Finally, I'll present a basic ritual for obtaining physical power. This ritual might be just what you need to assist you in making your physical body as healthy as possible. It does no good to obtain power (or wealth) if you can't sit back and enjoy it in a physically healthy body. We'll be using Astaroth in her goddess form. If you later seek a personal trainer, you may even attract someone who resembles the goddess in physical form. If you do, try not to mention how they remind you of a goddess. It'll just be too weird.

With each ritual, decide if you will work it as a Pathworking, or as a Ceremonial Ritual. For ease of use, I will present BOTH rituals in each sequence. This way, you do not have to flip back and forth through the book to work the pathworking rituals.

Also, make sure to use the Master Power Sigil. Have it with you as well as Astaroth's sigil and any sigil you may create using your statement of desire.

15

The Shield of Protection Ritual

If you are going to begin to achieve power, you will attract all sorts of attention. Some will be desired, wanted and helpful attention. The other type of attention is not desired, and that is the attention of potential enemies.

This part of the sequence has two options.

Simple, and effective shielding from attacking energy.

Then countering the attacking energy.

It is totally up to you which you can deploy. You may even decide that the person attacking you needs a dose of their own medicine.

In each circumstance, Astaroth has the power to protect you no matter who is behind the attacks. If it's a political-based attack, the counter attack can uncover their own foibles, forcing them to retreat and cease the attacks. Another excellent counter attack is to remove their ability to project and work magick.

For this, we'll be asking Astaroth to do two things: Remove anyone else's ability to attack you, either physically, with words, or energetically. We'll work with her as the Daemoness Astaroth.

The difference is in the wording of the petition.

Shielding: "Oh Astaroth! I ask that you now place an impenetrable shield around me, to defeat and deflect all energy attacks. I ask that this shield be perpetual, and require no more of my attention."

Dealing with attacks: "Oh Astaroth, I am the target of (verbal, written, or energy/magick) attack! I ask that you shield and protect me, and I further ask that you seek out the source of these attacks, and work to make the attacks cease, up to and including removing the attacking person's magick, or status, that allows them to engage in attacking me!"

Ceremonial Ritual for Shielding

This is identical to the basic daemonic ritual to Astaroth.

For this ritual, you will need the following specific candles:

- Two small black candles
- Black salt (*see appendix)
- Magick Ink
- Small sheet of paper
- Light mineral oil
- Offering of an egg, burnt meat, or your own drop of blood
- Astaroth's Daemon Sigil

Assemble your materials. Dress the black candles with the oil, any oil, I prefer light mineral oil. After dressing the candles, coat them with the black salt.

Using the magick ink, write your petition to Astaroth. Once the petition is written, allow the ink to dry and prepare yourself for the ritual.

Work the ritual as follows:

Light incense. Light altar candles, wait on lighting the black candles.

Room lights off

Cast your circle

Summon Astaroth using her ENN, said three times;

> *Tasa Alora foren Ashtaroth*
> *Tasa Alora foren Ashtaroth*
> *Tasa Alora foren Ashtaroth*
> *Astaroth, Daemon of Power*
> *Astaroth, Daemon of Wealth*
> *I ask that you join with me in my space*
> *Drink with me! Commune with me!*
> *Astaroth, it is my deepest desire that —*
> Read your petition

Astaroth, I ask that you bring to me what I have requested in this petition.

Prepare the offering. If an egg or meat, place it on her sigil and say

Astaroth, in gratitude I give to you this humble offering.

If offering blood say:

Astaroth, I now sacrifice my living essence to you,

In gratitude for acting on my petition.

At this point, prick your finger (any finger) with the diabetic lancet and allow a single drop of blood to land on her sigil. Hold the sigil up and touch it to the flame of her candle, and say:

To you, I give over this essence, Astaroth.

As the sigil burns, drop it into the fireproof container and make sure it burns completely. Stir the ashes to make sure it's totally consumed. After the ritual, toss the ashes outside, allowing them to be spread with the wind.

Time to finish the ritual. Place the petition or sigil on the altar and hold your hands over it. Take a moment to visualize energy flowing into the petition or sigil.

Oh Astaroth, please charge this (sigil or petition) with your energy, mix your energy with mine and work to make this manifest - so it is written, so it is done.

I thank you for being here with me, Astaroth, and you may now depart and please come again when I next call upon you!

The ritual is finished. Allow the black candles to burn out completely. Dispose of the leftover wax and ash in any manner you desire.

Pathworking Ritual for Shielding

Work this at a time when you know you'll not be disturbed.

As with the ceremonial ritual, you should write out a petition.

When ready, lower room lights and relax.

Visualize the pathworking:

- o An open country garden.
- o The smell of fresh flowers. Watch as a Honeysuckle blooms, and opens up.
- o Bluebirds land on a branch above you. See its red breast and bright blue back.
- o A warm, fresh breeze hits your face.

When Astaroth arrives, tell her of your need to protect yourself. Tell her everything. Then pause to listen to what she might say to you.

Visualize your petition. Open your eyes and read over your written petition.

As an offering, ask her what she might wish. As you are working with her in her daemoness form, she could ask for most anything. If she requests blood, do know you will have to actually prick a finger and place a drop onto her Daemonic Sigil, then burn it.

Once the offering is discussed and completed, ask her to leave using the usual phrase:

"Astaroth, thank you for your time with me, and you may depart, and please come again when I next call on you."

You can consider the ritual complete at this time.

Tracking success

Tracking the success of verbal attacks is quite easy. Tracking energy attacks a little harder. With verbal or written attacks, after these rituals you should begin to see people coming to your defense, and the attacks tapering off. Sometimes the people attacking you will be discredited.

In one situation I was in, the energy attacks seemed to continue until the person working the magick was openly discredited, and lost his power base of "students". He was unmasked and left the scene. This did take a while, about six weeks. After knowing this person was no longer able to attack me (or others), I have continued to monitor for signs of any renewed attacks.

Sometimes, it's wise to ask Astaroth to allow the attacking energy to bend around you, and have this energy appear to work, sending up the illusion of success. In this way, the attacking magician will *think* their attacks are working. If it appears that you have successfully countered the magick, the magicians' friends might assist. These people are, if anything, fanatical in their anger aimed at others. It's weird, but a lot of folks in the magick communities just love to get angry and hold grudges, and they're always being attacked or defending against attacks. I'm not a psychologist, but I am sure there's some mental problems that need attention with these people. I suppose it's like the super-religious crowds who are always crying that they're being attacked by their devil, egged on by the leaders of these groups. The way I look at it, that's not my circus and those are not my clowns.

16

Ritual to Project Charm and Charisma

Part of having power is the ability to sway people around to your point of view. Power is often granted to people from others. To make this happen, you may have to debate another person, present your case, and sway decision makers to see you in a highly favorable light.

Projecting charm is the way to get power. Developing charisma will bring many people to your side, and being able to project both while talking to them will pull them to your side of the argument or debate.

This is powerful magick to have on your side.

The petition needs to be worded such that you can invoke this ability at will. I'd write the petition using such phrases as "Please grant me the power of charisma, so that I may project confidence, leadership, and charm, causing people to easily follow me and allow me to lead them." Or "Please grant me the power of charm, so that everyone I meet will welcome me with smiles and open arms." If you intend to go into sales or politics, you could phrase the petition like this: "Please grant me the power of charisma, so that the people I meet will welcome me with open arms and open purses or wallets."

A side note on ethics is needed here. Astaroth, unlike Satan or Lilith, will not allow you to do any harm to the people you will use this power on. Make sure you deal with your audience honestly. Otherwise, use the next ritual on Projecting Power.

We will summon Astaroth in her Goddess aspect.

Ceremonial Ritual to Goddess Astaroth

You'll need the following items:

- Altar candles
- Astaroth's dedicated Goddess Candle
- Astaroth's Goddess Sigil
- Master Power Sigil
- Incense. Either frankincense resin or a stick of honeysuckle or lilac.
- Offering and offering bowl
- Red or Pink candle to represent your desire
- Your Petition
- Optional items: Crystals, Goblet of Water, Athame

Of the items above, you can make substitutions, such as essential oils for incense, and fake LED type candles for actual candles. Offerings should be fresh flowers, mead, red wine, or heavy cream with honey.

The Ritual

Gather up all materials needed. Have your petition written out, and the sigil if you have turned your desire into a sigil. Select a specific candle for this ritual.

When ready, light the incense and candles. If you are using charcoal and resin, make sure to get that charcoal puck going. It should be covered in white ash before starting the ritual.

Drop some incense onto the glowing charcoal, and cast your circle. If you are using a temporary altar space, make sure to work the Banishment as well, to eject any non-beneficial energy from your space.

Here are the basic steps in an easy-to-follow list:

> Light incense and candles
>
> Cast your circle
>
> Sit and meditate for a moment.
>
> Now call to Astaroth

> *Astaroth! Goddess of Life, Goddess of the Field, Goddess of the Hearth.*

> *Astaroth, you who have been known by name names,*

> *Astarte, Iananna, Venus, and others,*
>
> *Join with me in my space, talk with me,*
>
> *Grace me with your divine presence.*

> *Astaroth! I call to you now in your form as a Loving Goddess.*

> Pause a moment - stretch out your awareness to see if she is near you now.

Astaroth, I now ask that -
(Read your petition)

Pause now, and visualize the outcome of your desire manifesting. Run a daydream where it all occurs for you in the way you wish for it to manifest. Take your time doing this. (Hint: This is actually the key to how it all works.)

If you are using a special candle, pick it up now and say:

Oh, Goddess Astaroth! Please bless this candle to bring to me my desire!

Light the candle and set it into its holder.
Pick up your offering and now say:

Oh Astaroth, please accept this humble offering, in gratitude for listening to my petition.

Place the offering into the offering bowl, and place that on her sigil.

Now, time to charge the petition and all sigils with energy. Imagine gold energy pouring out of your hands. Then hold your hands over the petition and sigils and say the following:

Intro this petition, I now direct great power, power from you, Astaroth, and my own inner power, to make this desire manifest. And so it is!

After a minute or two, the petition or sigil is charged.

Oh, Goddess Astaroth, our time now is done. I thank you for your presence in my circle.

You may depart peacefully now and please return when I next call upon you!

At this point, you can walk out of the circle.

Keep your sigil or petition near you for the next few days. You can place it under a pillow, or in a wallet or purse.

The next day, discard the offering outside.

Pathworking Ritual to Goddess Astaroth

Prepare yourself and your space for this ritual. Lower the room lights, and if using any candles, light those. Have your petition and Master Power Sigil handy.

When ready, visualize the following:

- A hot day, with no clouds in the sky.
- An oasis in the desert, surrounded by goats and camels.
- A beautiful woman approaches you, her face covered in a veil.
- The woman's eyes stare at you, then she blinks.
- You are now inside an ancient temple, tan rock walls.
- Smoke surrounds you.

At this point, Astaroth will appear to you.

When the goddess appears, greet her by projecting your words to her. You can also whisper if you wish, but mental projection works just as well.

Visualize your desire. Go into as much detail as you can, making it a mental movie.

What will it feel like when this desire manifests? Hold onto this emotion.

After a few moments with this visualization, ask Astaroth to assist you in making this manifest, reading your petition.

Be silent for a minute or two, then ask the Goddess if she has anything to tell you.

Send her a brief burst of pink light. Imagine this pink light going from the top of your head and into Astaroth's body. This is loving light of gratitude.

Tell her goodbye, and any other positive phrases you wish to tell her.

Breathe a bit, then a cleansing breath. Open your eyes. The ritual is finished.

17

Project Aura of Power Ritual

Projection of power is just as important as charisma. You can be charming as the most successful game show host, but if you can't project it, you are not reaching everyone.

Since this type of magick involves altering how people receive you, we'll use Astaroth the daemon.

Candles. Basic altar candles can be any color. I prefer white and black. Use a red candle for Astaroth in her daemonic aspect. It's totally optional to draw her sigil on this red candle. If so, use silver, as that looks really cool.

Incense and Incense burner.

- Astaroth's Candle
- Astaroth's Sigil for her daemon form
- The Master Power Sigil
- Go with a red candle for power, or yellow for communication.
- Offering bowl.
- Offering
- Fireproof bowl, as you will burn the petition.

- Optional items: Crystals, alternatives to incense such as essential oils, and alternatives to candles such as LED candles.

To start, gather up all the needed materials. Then:

Light the incense and candles (except for the desire candle).

Lights off.

Cast your circle and run the Banishing of the Pentagram if it is needed.

Settle yourself in and relax.

Breathe deeply and allow yourself to go into a slight trance state.

Meditate for a moment on the goal of the ritual, and read over the petition you plan to use.

Now, summon Astaroth, saying her common ENN three times.

Tasa Alora foren Ashtaroth

Tasa Alora foren Ashtaroth

Tasa Alora foren Ashtaroth

Astaroth, Daemon of Power

Astaroth, Daemon of Wealth

I ask that you join with me in my space

Join with me! Be with me! Commune with me!

Astaroth, it is my deepest desire that —

Read your petition

Astaroth, I ask that you bring to me what I have requested in this petition.

Hold up the red power candle now, and say:

Astaroth, I ask that you now bless this candle so that it will bring to me my desire.

(Light the candle and make sure it's in a safe location)

And in gratitude for your assistance and for being here to listen to my prayer,
I hereby give to you this humble _____ (the offering if it is **NOT** a blood offering)

If you are giving her a blood offering, say the following after thanking her for listening to your petition:
Astaroth, I now sacrifice my living essence to you,
In gratitude for acting on my petition.

At this point, prick your finger (any finger) with the diabetic lancet and allow a single drop of blood to land on her sigil. Hold the sigil up and touch it to the flame of her candle, and say:

To you, I give over this essence, Astaroth.

As the sigil burns, drop it into the fireproof container and make sure it burns completely. Stir the ashes to make sure it's totally consumed. After the ritual, toss the ashes outside, allowing them to be spread with the wind.

Time to finish the ritual. Place the petition and sigil on the altar and hold your hands over it. Visualize red energy forming around your hands. Hold your hands over the petition and sigils, then visualize the red energy flowing into the petition and sigil.

> *Oh Astaroth, please charge this sigil and petition with your energy, mix your energy with mine and work to make this manifest - so it is written, so it is done.*
> *I thank you for being here with me, Astaroth, and you may now depart and please come again when I next call upon you!*

That pretty much wraps up this ritual.

If offering something other than blood, allow this offering to stay on your altar, on her sigil, until the following day, then take it outside and place the offering into nature. If it's an offering of wine or spirit, pour the offering out onto the ground.

Pathworking for Power Aura and Projection

Work this at a time when you know you'll not be disturbed.

As with the ceremonial ritual, you should write out a petition. Also have your Master Power Sigil handy.

When ready, lower room lights and relax.

Visualize the pathworking:
- o An open country garden.
- o The smell of fresh flowers. Watch as a Honeysuckle blooms, and opens up.
- o Bluebirds land on a branch above you. See its red breast and bright blue back.

     o   A warm, fresh breeze hits your face.

When Astaroth arrives, tell her of your need to project power and possess the aura of power, and let her know what type of power you desire. Tell her everything. Then pause to listen to what she might say to you.

Visualize your petition. Open your eyes and read over your written petition. Now, simply gaze at the Master Power Sigil.

Then, meditate on this desire, and see it manifesting. Go into as much detail as you can, making it a mental movie.

What will it feel like when this desire manifests? Hold onto this emotion.

After a few moments with this visualization, ask Astaroth to assist you in making this manifest.

As an offering, ask her what she might wish. As you are working with her in her daemoness form, she could ask for most anything. If she requests blood, do know you will have to actually prick a finger and place a drop onto her Daemonic Sigil, then burn it.

Once the offering is discussed and completed, ask her to leave using the usual phrase:

"Astaroth, thank you for your time with me, and you may depart, and please come again when I next call on you."

You can consider the ritual complete at this time.

18

Ritual of the Silver Tongue

Sometimes, in order to sell yourself or your position, you need listeners to really listen and begin to follow what you are saying. This ritual will cause your listeners to fall into a trance-like state and be easily led. This will assist you in gaining political power over others. Just be careful with this one.

Obviously, we'll be using Astaroth in her daemoness form for this set of rituals. Suggested petition states would be "Astaroth! Please enchant my tongue, giving me the power of the Silver Tongue, so that my listeners will be filled with a desire to follow me, acting on my advice, joining with me, or buying what I am selling."

- Incense and Incense burner.
- Go with a silver candle for this ritual.
- Offering bowl.
- Offering
- Fireproof bowl, as you will burn the petition.
- Optional items: Crystals, alternatives to incense such

as essential oils, and alternatives to candles such as LED candles.

To start, gather up all the needed materials. Then:

Light the incense and candles (except for the desire candle).

Lights off.

Cast your circle and run the Banishing of the Pentagram if it is needed.

Settle yourself in and relax.

Breathe deeply and allow yourself to go into a slight trance state.

Meditate for a moment on the goal of the ritual, and read over the petition you plan to use.

Now, summon Astaroth, saying her common ENN three times.

Tasa Alora foren Ashtaroth

Tasa Alora foren Ashtaroth

Tasa Alora foren Ashtaroth

Astaroth, Daemon of Power

Astaroth, Daemon of Wealth

I ask that you join with me in my space

Join with me! Be with me! Commune with me!

Astaroth, it is my deepest desire that —

Read your petition

Astaroth, I ask that you bring to me what I have requested in this petition.

(If burning an additional candle for this desire, take hold of it now)

Astaroth, I ask that you now bless this candle so that it will bring to me my desire.

(Light the candle and make sure it's in a safe location)

And in gratitude for your assistance and for being here to listen to my prayer,
I hereby give to you this humble _____ (the offering if it is **NOT** a blood offering)

If you are giving her a blood offering, say the following after thanking her for listening to your petition:
Astaroth, I now sacrifice my living essence to you,
In gratitude for acting on my petition.

At this point, prick your finger (any finger) with the diabetic lancet and allow a single drop of blood to land on her sigil. Hold the sigil up and touch it to the flame of her candle, and say:

To you, I give over my essence, Astaroth.

As the sigil burns, drop it into the fireproof container and make sure it burns completely. Stir the ashes to make sure it's totally consumed. After the ritual, toss the ashes outside, allowing them to be spread with the wind.

Time to finish the ritual. Place the petition or sigil on the altar and hold your hands over it. Take a moment to visualize energy flowing into the petition or sigil.

Oh Astaroth, please charge this (sigil or petition) with your energy, mix your energy with mine and work to make this manifest - so it is written, so it is done.

I thank you for being here with me, Astaroth, and you may now depart and please come again when I next call upon you!

That pretty much wraps up this ritual.

If offering something other than blood, allow this offering to stay on your altar, on her sigil, until the following day, then take it outside and place the offering into nature. If it's an offering of wine or spirit, pour the offering out onto the ground.

Pathworking for Power Aura and Projection

Work this at a time when you know you'll not be disturbed.

As with the ceremonial ritual, you should write out a petition.

When ready, lower room lights and relax.

- Visualize the pathworking:
- An open country garden.
- The smell of fresh flowers. Watch as a Honeysuckle blooms, and opens up.
- Bluebirds land on a branch above you. See its red breast and bright blue back.
- A warm, fresh breeze hits your face.

When Astaroth arrives, tell her of your need to project power and possess the aura of power, and let her know what type of power you desire. Tell her everything. Then pause to listen to what she might say to you.

Visualize your petition. Open your eyes and read over your written petition.

Then, meditate on this desire, and see it manifesting. Go into as much detail as you can, making it a mental movie.

What will it feel like when this desire manifests? Hold onto this emotion.

After a few moments with this visualization, ask Astaroth to assist you in making this manifest.

As an offering, ask her what she might wish. As you are working with her in her daemoness form, she could ask for most anything. If she requests blood, do know you will have to actually prick a finger and place a drop onto her Daemonic Sigil, then burn it.

Once the offering is discussed and completed, ask her to leave using the usual phrase:

"Astaroth, thank you for your time with me, and you may depart, and please come again when I next call on you."

You can consider the ritual complete at this time.

19

Ritual for Physical Health and Power

This is powerful magick to use when getting into shape.

The petition needs to be worded such that you encourage the cells in your body to gain strength. Suggested wording can be: "I ask that you grant me the ability to achieve optimum health and begin to gain strength rapidly while I exercise."

Make sure to actually exercise. Astaroth as a goddess can work miracles, but you do need to meet her half-way. Get off the couch and put down the sugary breakfast cereal and go to the gym.

We will summon Astaroth in her Goddess aspect.

Ceremonial Ritual to Goddess Astaroth

You'll need the following items:

- Altar candles
- Astaroth's dedicated Goddess Candle
- Astaroth's Goddess Sigil
- Incense. Either frankincense resin or a stick of

honeysuckle or lilac.

- Offering and offering bowl
- Blue or Purple candle to represent health and healing
- Your Petition
- Optional items: Crystals, Goblet of Water, Athame

Of the items above, you can make substitutions, such as essential oils for incense, and fake LED type candles for actual candles. Offerings should be fresh flowers, mead, red wine, or heavy cream with honey.

The Ritual

Gather up all materials needed. Have your petition written out, and the sigil if you have turned your desire into a sigil. Select a specific candle for this ritual.

When ready, light the incense and candles. If you are using charcoal and resin, make sure to get that charcoal puck going. It should be covered in white ash before starting the ritual.

Drop some incense onto the glowing charcoal, and cast your circle. If you are using a temporary altar space, make sure to work the Banishment as well, to eject any non-beneficial energy from your space.

Here are the basic steps in an easy to follow list:

Light incense and candles

Cast your circle

Sit and meditate for a moment.

Now call to Astaroth

Astaroth! Goddess of Life, Goddess of the Field,

Goddess of the Hearth.

> *Astaroth, you who have been known by name names,*

> *Astarte, Iananna, Venus, and others,*
> *Join with me in my space, talk with me,*
> *Grace me with your divine presence.*

> *Astaroth! I call to you now in your form as a Loving Goddess.*

Pause a moment - stretch out your awareness to see if she is near you now.

> *Astaroth, I now ask that -*
> (Read your petition)

Pause now, and visualize the outcome of your desire manifesting. Run a daydream where it all occurs for you in the way you wish for it to manifest. Take your time doing this. (Hint: This is actually the key to how it all works.)

If you are using a special candle, pick it up now and say:

> *Oh, Goddess Astaroth! Please bless this candle to bring to me my desire!*

Light the candle and set it into its holder.
Pick up your offering and now say:

> *Oh Astaroth, please accept this humble offering, in*

gratitude for listening to my petition.

Place the offering into the offering bowl, and place that on her sigil.

Now, time to charge the petition or sigil with energy. Hold your hands over the petition or sigil and say the following:

Intro this petition, I now direct great power, power from you, Astaroth, and my own inner power, to make this desire manifest. And so it is!

After a minute or two, the petition or sigil is charged.

Oh, Goddess Astaroth, our time now is done. I thank you for your presence in my circle.

You may depart peacefully now and please return when I next call upon you!

At this point, you can walk out of the circle.

Keep your sigil or petition near you for the next few days. You can place it under a pillow, or in a wallet or purse.

The next day, discard the offering outside.

Pathworking Ritual to Goddess Astaroth

Prepare yourself and your space for this ritual. Lower the room lights, and if using any candles, light those. Have your petition handy.

When ready, visualize the following:

- A hot day, with no clouds in the sky.
- An oasis in the desert, surrounded by goats and camels.
- A beautiful woman approaches you, her face covered in a veil.
- The woman's eyes stare at you, then she blinks.
- You are now inside an ancient temple, tan rock walls.
- Smoke surrounds you.

At this point, Astaroth will appear to you.

When the goddess appears, greet her by projecting your words to her. You can also whisper if you wish, but mental projection works just as well.

Visualize your desire. Go into as much detail as you can, making it a mental movie.

What will it feel like when this desire manifests? Hold onto this emotion.

After a few moments with this visualization, ask Astaroth to assist you in making this manifest, reading your petition.

Be silent for a minute or two, then ask Astaroth if she has anything to tell you.

Send her a brief burst of pink light. Imagine this pink light going from the top of your head and into Astaroth's body. This is loving light of gratitude.

Tell her goodbye, and any other positive phrases you wish to tell her.

Breathe a bit, then a cleansing breath. Open your eyes. The

ritual is finished.

20

Wealth Sequence

It is recommended to work through all the following rituals in order.

Step One: Release Blocks

I often find students trying to work money magick while carrying many blocks. The first ritual is to release those blocks. Often, blocks are internal, but sometimes I find actual external blocks. In those cases, I recommend a road opening ritual. This ritual combines *both.*

The removing blocks ritual may have to be worked multiple times. Although you can work it on any day of the week or month, you may find working it during the suggested days or times beneficial.

For blocks releasing, you would want to work on a Sunday or Monday, using the energy of the Sun or Moon to help clear blocks. Work between the day after the full moon, to the day before the new moon. Of all the celestial energies used in magick, the moon is the most useful, and my experiences indicate this is very useful.

Step Two: Opening up to Receive.

The inability to receive can be considered an internal block. This is when, although you need a new job or a windfall, you somehow feel you do NOT deserve this to come into your life.

Step Three: Income Streams and Income Boosting

Then, we will ask Astaroth to generate multiple sources for income and money to flow to you. It's not wise to "put all your eggs (or any poultry product, for that matter) into a single basket". Diversify. Truly wealthy people have multiple projects, businesses, investments in many different industries and companies. This way, if one channel suddenly tanks, you have other areas to make up for the losses.

The Wealth Sequence

We'll start with blocks.

Many of the people I have assisted have internal blocks when it comes to money. This is often from a life of having no money, which impresses on your mind the idea that "We're Poor". This mindset can cause someone with a fantastic job to figure out a way to sabotage themselves and wind up getting fired.

I see this almost every day. Going shopping for food, and getting upset at the high prices, instead of going shopping and being relaxed, knowing you can afford that high priced package of imported cheese.

If you just thought something like "Hell, only people who buy that are lucky people!", then you got an enormous block and it needs to be released.

It's that subtle. It's also hidden from plain view.

But you can trick your subconscious into making wealth a reality by simply going forth with a new attitude of "Hell yeah, let's buy the very best!"

Yes, it's difficult. I should know, I have had my own inner blocks for a long time. A few years ago, I recognized what was happening, and I could stop it. It took several different block removal rituals. I eventually wrote one that combined the different aspects of some others, and this is the ritual you will be working.

But, I hear some of ya'll saying "Dave! I don't have any blocks, it's just that —"

Hold on, partner! The second you said "It's just that…" you revealed a block.

Thus, two of the three wealth rituals are all about clearing blocks and opening yourself to being able to receive. The two work hand in paw. Or paw in paw, depending on the type of inner daemon you have. Mine has paws that have sharp claws. Actually, his hands are more like talons.

So, after blocks are cleared, we move onto *Opening up to Receive.*

Are you the type who, when given a present for a special occasion, always wants to refuse the gift? I don't mean someone who says, "Aww, you didn't have to!" then rips into the package with glee, but the person who inside cringes because you find it hard to accept a gift? This even includes compliments!

Realizing how to receive can even open you up to relationships with new lovers! Trust me, it's very effective in all areas of your life.

21

Step One: Releasing Inner and/or External Blocks

This ritual is to the daemon aspect of Astaroth.

For this one, I highly recommend a combination reverse candle (red/black) and an orange candle for opening up pathways.

The petition should be worded in such a way as to combine both desired results into a single request. I suggest a phrasing like: "Astaroth! I ask that you assist me in removing all the barriers to gaining wealth. Help me resolve any internal issues I have that prevents me from moving forward and obtaining great wealth. I also ask that you clear my path of any outside interference and blocks that may be in place!"

Be prepared to offer Astaroth a small blood sacrifice. If you create a sigil for this, you should also draw it on the orange candle. After drawing the sigil, you should coat the candle with black salt. Using a light oil, coat the candle, then roll it in a small amount of black salt.

If you are using a reverse candle, after getting it, "reverse" it before this ritual. To do this, carefully cut the top off, making the top level. Then turn the candle upside down, cut at the bottom to free up the wick, then coat the candle in oil, and roll it in black salt.

If you want, you can also obtain a glass votive candle, a "7-day" candle, in orange. Draw the sigils on the glass, then also drop some "Road Opening" oil on the candle. Road opening oil can be obtained online.

The Ritual

Light the incense and altar candles (except for the desire candle).

Lights off.

Cast your circle and run the Banishing of the Pentagram if it is needed.

Settle yourself in and relax.

Breathe deeply and allow yourself to go into a slight trance state.

Meditate for a moment on the goal of the ritual, and read over the petition you plan to use.

Now, summon Astaroth, saying her common ENN three times.

Tasa Alora foren Ashtaroth
Tasa Alora foren Ashtaroth
Tasa Alora foren Ashtaroth
Astaroth, Daemon of Power
Astaroth, Daemon of Wealth
I ask that you join with me in my space
Drink with me! Commune with me!
Astaroth, it is my deepest desire that —

Read your petition

Astaroth, I ask that you bring to me what I have requested in this petition.

Hold up the reversal or orange candle now.

Astaroth, I ask that you now bless this candle so that it will remove all blocks and energy holding me back from obtaining great wealth!

(Light the candle and make sure it's in a safe location)

And in gratitude for your assistance and for being here to listen to my prayer,

Astaroth, I now sacrifice my living essence to you,
In gratitude for acting on my petition.

Prick your finger (any finger) with the diabetic lancet and allow a single drop of blood to land on her sigil. Hold the sigil up and touch it to the flame of her candle, and say,

To you, I give over my essence, Astaroth.

As the sigil burns, drop it into the fireproof container and make sure it burns completely. Stir the ashes to make sure it's totally consumed. After the ritual, toss the ashes outside, allowing them to be spread with the wind.

Time to finish the ritual. Place the petition or sigil on the altar and hold your hands over it. Take a moment to visualize energy flowing into the petition or sigil.

Oh Astaroth, please charge this (sigil or petition)

with your energy, mix your energy with mine and work to make this manifest - so it is written, so it is done.

I thank you for being here with me, Astaroth, and you may now depart and please come again when I next call upon you!

Carefully, allow the candle to burn completely. Make sure it is burning in a safe place. The next day, remove any leftover wax and the ashes from the sacrifice, and put these into nature.

If burning the 7-day candle, allow it to completely burn out, then break up the glass into small pieces, and put them a small bag and then in the trash.

Optional: Find and print out a drawing or photo that represents "Poverty" to you. Then, before working this ritual, draw a bright red slash across the photo, and on the back, write: "I Banish Thee!"

In ritual, hold this up and focus on it, imagine banishing poverty once and for all. Then burn the photo, stirring it's ashes to make sure it's completely burned and banished.

22

Step Two: Opening to Receive

Yes, I know, it appears that "Opening to Receive" would work the same as "Block Removal". But not really. Opening up to receive isn't exactly the same as removing blocks. This is a fully internal issue and gently adjusts your reaction to receiving things. Such things as massive amounts of money.

By using this ritual, we can make sure all blocks are resolved.

For this, we will use the Goddess Astaroth. Pay attention when crafting your petition. Make sure the phrasing is positive and does not mention "blocks" or other words like obstacles and hindrances. Unlike removing blocks, this is designed to give you the power to pull your desire to you.

ANY desire.

So, I suggest you use phrases like this: "Open me up to receive all the money and wealth I desire." You can even say "deserve", or "have the right to receive." Not only does this direct how the magick will work, but what effect it will have on you and your subconscious. This is very important. The subconscious is responsible for 90% of all manifestations in your life. So, this is something we have to shift.

As a goddess, Astaroth's energy is soft and pushes gently. So much so, your subconscious will not know what is happening and won't fight against it. Astaroth can also engage with your subconscious self and persuade that inner voice to be quiet and allow the wealth to begin to flow to you.

For the full ritual, locate and use light blue or purple candles. An offering can be most anything, and I always use red wine as I have found this to be the best offering for any deity.

Also, print out and include the Master Wealth Sigil for this ritual as well.

Ceremonial Ritual Opening to Receive

Prepare your petition, gather the needed incense and special candles. If you have a custom sigil for this, place that on the altar. Arrange the altar in a way that best works for you.

Items needed:
- Frankincense or similar
- Light blue or purple candle
- Astaroth's Goddess Sigil
- Astaroth's Goddess candle
- Master Wealth Sigil

When ready, light the incense and candles. If you are using charcoal and resin, make sure to get that charcoal puck going. It should be covered in white ash before starting the ritual.

Drop some incense onto the glowing charcoal, and cast your

circle. If you are using a temporary altar space, be sure to work the Banishment as well, to eject any non-beneficial energy from your space.

Here are the basic steps in an easy-to-follow list:

Light incense and candles

Cast your circle

Sit and meditate for a moment.

Now call to Astaroth

Astaroth! Goddess of Life, Goddess of the Field, Goddess of the Hearth.

Astaroth, you who have been known by name names,

Astarte, Iananna, Venus, and others,

Join with me in my space, talk with me,

Grace me with your divine presence.

Astaroth! I call to you now in your form as a Loving Goddess.

Pause a moment - stretch out your awareness to see if she is near you now.

Astaroth, I now ask that -

(Read your petition)

Pause now, and visualize the outcome of your desire manifesting. Run a daydream where it all occurs for you in the way you wish for it to manifest. Take your time doing this. (Hint: This is actually the key to how it all works.)

Pick it up the light blue or purple candle now and

say:

Oh, Goddess Astaroth! Please bless this candle to dissolve any inner blocks I have.

Light the candle and set it into its holder.
Pick up the offering and now say:

Oh Astaroth, please accept this humble offering, in gratitude for listening to my petition.

Place the offering into the offering bowl, and place that on her sigil.

Now, time to charge the petition and sigil with energy. Imagine blue energy appearing in your hands, then hold your hands over the petition and sigil, then say the following:

Intro this petition and sigil, I now direct great power, power from you, Astaroth, and my own inner power, to make this desire manifest. And so it is!

After a minute or two, the petition or sigil is charged.

Oh, Goddess Astaroth, our time now is done. I thank you for your presence in my circle. You may depart peacefully now and please return when I next call upon you!

Allow the pale blue or purple candle to burn out and take the offering outside the next day and place it anywhere in nature.

Pathworking Opening to Receive

Prepare your petition and your space for this ritual. Lower the room lights, and if using any candles, light those. Have your petition handy and the Master Sigil handy.

When ready, visualize the following:

- A hot day, with no clouds in the sky.
- An oasis in the desert, surrounded by goats and camels.
- A beautiful woman approaches you, her face covered in a veil.
- The woman's eyes stare at you, then she blinks.
- You are now inside an ancient temple, tan rock walls.
- Smoke surrounds you.

At this point, Astaroth will appear to you.

When the goddess appears, greet her by projecting your words to her. You can also whisper if you wish, but mental projection works just as well.

Visualize your desire. Go into as much detail as you can, making it a mental movie.

What will it feel like when this desire manifests? Hold on to this emotion.

Now, gaze at the Master Wealth Sigil. Just gaze at it. Imagine it's power manifesting in your life, drawing wealth and good fortune to you.

After a few moments with this visualization, ask Astaroth to assist you in making this manifest, reading your petition.

Be silent for a minute or two, then ask the Goddess if she has anything to tell you.

Send her a brief burst of pink light. Imagine this pink light going from the top of your head and into Astaroth's body. This is loving light of gratitude.

Tell her goodbye, and any other positive phrases you wish to tell her.

Breathe a bit, then a cleansing breath. Open your eyes. The ritual is finished.

23

Step Three: Unlimited Income

Daemons make for some fantastic money magick. I'm not sure why, as I've had significant results with Fortuna, but Astaroth really rocks it when it comes to opening up avenues for additional income. That's the purpose of this ritual, opening up unlimited income sources.

From diversifying your sales to opening up new territories, this ritual works. As I ran this, it occurred to me to offer one of my books as a special edition hardback with a jacket. I used a new printing partner, and this book has been selling very well in physical bookstores, and has distribution worldwide.

So be open for guidance after working this ritual.

The petition.

Phrase it like "Astaroth, I ask that you now open up for me unlimited sources of new income, opportunities to generate more and more money and wealth!" "Every day, in every way, new sources of unlimited streams of income open up for me, and with your help, Astaroth, my wealth grows and grows!"

Ceremonial Ritual for Unlimited Income

For this ritual, you will need the usual altar space, and the following money-specific items:

- Gold or silver candles, you can use green in a pinch.
- Money specific incense. Frankincense and Myrrh are traditional luxury incenses, so use them.
- Astaroth's Daemon Sigil and specific candle
- The Master Wealth Sigil.
- Optional items: Crystals, alternatives to incense such as essential oils, and alternatives to candles such as LED candles. You can also include specific oils for money, such as money-drawing oil, crown of success, etc.

When ready, make sure you have everything you need next to you. If you forget the petition, for example, (like I do) you'll need to cast your circle again after moving out of it.

Light the incense and candles (except for the desire candle).

Lights off.

Cast your circle and run the Banishing of the Pentagram if it is needed.

Settle yourself in and relax.

Breathe deeply and allow yourself to go into a slight trance state.

Meditate for a moment on the goal of the ritual, and read over the petition you plan to use.

Now, summon Astaroth, saying her common ENN

three times.

>*Tasa Alora foren Ashtaroth*
>*Tasa Alora foren Ashtaroth*
>*Tasa Alora foren Ashtaroth*
>*Astaroth, Daemon of Power*
>*Astaroth, Daemon of Wealth*
>*I ask that you join with me in my space*
>*Be with me! Commune with me!*
>*Astaroth, it is my deepest desire that —*
>Read your petition
>*Astaroth, I ask that you bring to me what I have requested in this petition.*

Hold up the gold (or silver) candle, and say:

>*Astaroth, I ask that you now bless this candle so that it will bring to me my desire.*

(Light the candle and make sure it's in a safe location)

>*And in gratitude for your assistance and for being here to listen to my prayer,*
>*I hereby give to you this humble* _____ (the offering if it is **NOT** a blood offering)

If you are giving her a blood offering, say the following after thanking her for listening to your petition:

>*Astaroth, I now sacrifice my living essence to you,*
>*In gratitude for acting on my petition.*

At this point, prick your finger (any finger) with the diabetic lancet and allow a single drop of blood to land on her sigil. Hold the sigil up and touch it to the flame of her candle, and say:

To you, I give over my essence, Astaroth.

As the sigil burns, drop it into the fireproof container and make sure it burns completely. Stir the ashes to make sure it's totally consumed. After the ritual, toss the ashes outside, allowing them to be spread with the wind.

Time to finish the ritual. Place the petition or sigil on the altar and hold your hands over it. Imagine seeing gold energy forming around your hands. Take a moment to visualize this golden energy flowing into the petition and sigil.

Oh Astaroth, please charge this sigil and petition with your energy, mix your energy with mine and work to make this manifest - so it is written, so it is done.

I thank you for being here with me, Astaroth, and you may now depart and please come again when I next call upon you!

That pretty much wraps up this ritual.

If offering something other than blood, allow this offering to stay on your altar, on her sigil, until the following day, then take it outside and place the offering into nature. If it's an offering of wine or spirit, pour the offering out onto the ground.

Pathworking Unlimited Income

Work this when you know you'll not be disturbed.

As with the ceremonial ritual, write out a petition. Have it and the Master Wealth Sigil with you.

When ready, lower room lights and relax.

Visualize the pathworking:

- An open country garden.
- The smell of fresh flowers. Watch as a Honeysuckle blooms, and opens up.
- Bluebirds land on a branch above you. See its red breast and bright blue back.
- A warm, fresh breeze hits your face.

When Astaroth arrives, tell her of your need to project power and possess the aura of power, and let her know your desire for unlimited sources of income to appear for you. Tell her everything. Let her know what plans you have for this wealth. Then pause to listen to what she might say to you.

Visualize your petition. Open your eyes and read over your written petition.

Then meditate on this desire, and see it manifesting. Go into as much detail as you can, making it a mental movie.

What will it feel like when this desire manifests? Hold on to this emotion.

Now, gaze at the Master Wealth Sigil. Watch as the design begins to glow.

After a few moments with this visualization, ask Astaroth to assist you in making this manifest.

As an offering, ask her what she might wish. As you are working with her in her daemoness form, she could ask for most anything. If she requests blood, know you will have to actually prick a finger and place a drop onto her Daemonic Sigil, then burn it.

Once the offering is discussed and completed, ask her to leave using the usual phrase:

"Astaroth, thank you for your time with me, and you may depart, and please come again when I next call on you."

You can consider the ritual complete.

24

General Purpose Income Ritual

Straight forward. Use this for when you feel your income stream needs a boost. It's a "General Purpose" ritual, and the details will be in your petition.

Word your petition so that money begins to flow to you. Do not limit its source, or its amount. A good petition can read: "Astaroth, I ask that you now boost the money flowing into my life. In amounts which increase day after day, growing strong and stronger, money flow without end."

Of course, use gold or silver candles. Green if you can't find the gold candles. Use a money-drawing oil if you have it handy. Anoint the gold candle and place it on your altar.

Have the Master Wealth Sigil with you as well.

When ready, light the incense and candles. If you are using charcoal and resin, make sure to get that charcoal puck going. It should be covered in white ash before starting the ritual.

Drop some incense onto the glowing charcoal, and cast your circle. If you are using a temporary altar space, be sure to work the Banishment as well, to eject any non-beneficial energy from your space.

Here are the basic steps in an easy-to-follow list:

Light incense and candles

Cast your circle

Sit and meditate for a moment.

Now call to Astaroth

Astaroth! Goddess of Life, Goddess of the Field, Goddess of the Hearth.

Astaroth, you who have been known by name names,

Astarte, Iananna, Venus, and others,

Join with me in my space, talk with me,

Grace me with your divine presence.

Astaroth! I call to you now in your form as a Loving Goddess.

Pause a moment - stretch out your awareness to see if she is near you now.

Astaroth, I now ask that -

(Read your petition)

Pause now, and visualize the outcome of your desire manifesting. Run a daydream where it all occurs for you in the way you wish for it to manifest. Take your time doing this. (Hint: This is actually the key to how it all works.)

Pick up the gold candle and say:

Oh, Goddess Astaroth! Please bless this candle to bring me more and more money, in ever-increasing amounts!

Light the candle and set it into its holder.
Pick up the offering and now say:

Oh Astaroth, please accept this humble offering, in gratitude for listening to my petition.

Place the offering into the offering bowl, and place the bowl on her sigil.

Now, time to charge the petition and sigil with energy. Hold your hands over the petition and sigil, imagine bright golden or silver energy flowing from your hands and into the petition and sigil. Now say the following:

Into this sigil and petition, I direct great power, power from you, Astaroth, and my inner power, to make this desire manifest. And so it is!

After a minute or two, the petition or sigil is charged.

Oh, Goddess Astaroth, our time now is done. I thank you for your presence in my circle. You may depart peacefully now and please return when I next call upon you!

Allow the offering to stay on the altar overnight. The gold candle will need to burn until it goes out on its own.

Pathworking General Income Increase

Give a lot of thought to the petition. Make sure it's how you want it.

When ready, lower the room lights, and if using any candles, light those. Have your petition and the Master Wealth Sigil handy.

Begin by visualizing the following:

- A hot day, with no clouds in the sky.
- An oasis in the desert, surrounded by goats and camels.
- A beautiful woman approaches you, her face covered in a veil.
- The woman's eyes stare at you, then she blinks.
- You are now inside an ancient temple, tan rock walls.
- Smoke surrounds you.

At this point, Astaroth will appear to you.

When the goddess appears, greet her by projecting your words to her. You can also whisper if you wish, but mental projection works just as well.

Visualize your desire. Go into as much detail as you can, making it a mental movie.

What will it feel like when this desire manifests? Hold on to this emotion.

Now, look at the Wealth Sigil. Just gaze at it, allowing the images to shift in focus. Again, see your desire manifesting.

After a few moments with this visualization, ask Astaroth to assist you in making this manifest, reading your petition.

Be silent for a minute or two, then ask the Goddess if she has anything to tell you.

Send her a brief burst of pink light. Imagine this pink light going from the top of your head and into Astaroth's body. This is loving light of gratitude.

Tell her goodbye, and any other positive phrases you wish to tell her.

Breathe a bit, then a cleansing breath. Open your eyes. The ritual is finished.

25

Pacts

First, let's get some myths out of the way.

One: You cannot sell your soul to any daemon. Entering into a pact doesn't trade your soul for anything. If it did, I assure you I would have found and married the daughter of a famous film producer way back in the 1980s.

Two: It's not dangerous. At least, no more dangerous than any other magical working. It certainly carries less risk than walking along a city sidewalk. Definitely less risk than flying on a Boeing 737 Max.

A pact is for a long-term goal, such as the non-violent overthrow of the bourgeoisie in your current city or country. (Though, those tend to get messy even if non-violent.) Starting a new business and setting it up for steady growth is a wonderful goal for a pact.

In a pact, you ask the spirit to assist you in a specific goal, and then you specify what you will do in return for the spirit. I did this for my best-selling book on Fortuna. I released that one months ago, and it's still selling quite strongly. So, it achieved the pact's goals of promoting Fortuna, and giving me a best-selling book.

A pact needs to be written differently than a simple petition, as there will need to be goal setting, and what will happen if the spirit does not assist you in actually achieving your goal? Spirits like daemons or gods/goddesses have some limitations. (If you want someone with unlimited ability to shift the world, go look at daemons like Sorath or a creator-level spirit like "The Avatar") However, YOU also have to put a lot of time and energy into this goal. It does no good to ask for endless wealth if you prefer to sit around all day watching the Game Show channel on a streaming service.

Writing your pact is simple: Using magick ink, write the pact statement out by hand, and leave it unsigned until time for the pact ritual. I use a small piece of plain paper, and I make my magick ink. It's really easy. I have several fountain pens and lots of bottled ink. I will take a small clean ink bottle, pour an ounce of ink into it, then poke myself with a diabetic lancet and drop some of my blood into the ink, cap it carefully and shake. Magick ink!

I use a cheap fountain pen I found on a "popular internet auction site", usually a brand called Jinhao. I will dip the pen into the ink and write out the pact statement. I will also have this pen with me during the ritual. I have not tried to load the pen with the magick ink, as adding blood makes the ink thicker, so it will likely clog the pen itself. Always rinse the fountain pet with water after using it. Or that ink will dry and it'll be hard to use again.

You could buy a small calligraphy pen kit and use that.

Whichever is easiest for you.

Choose a fine point and write the pact out carefully. My handwriting is pretty bad. So much so, I once had a doctor ask me what I'd written down. She couldn't make it out. Jokes ensued. The nurses even mentioned my bad handwriting during my next appointment. They love a good joke.

During the pact ritual, after reading the pact, you will sign the pact itself. I often will add a drop of blood to the pack if I am working with a daemon, as a way to seal the pact. Some suggest also adding the daemon's sigil to the bottom. If so, add a drop of blood onto it as well.

There is a debate among many whether to burn the pack afterwards, as you would a blood offering, or keep the pact and hide it under the bed or in a drawer. I have done this both ways, and I can't see a difference.

A pact with a daemon is different from a pact with a deity, as you will see, but the difference is quite minor. The major difference is in offerings and using blood drops as a signature. Don't offer blood to a deity, as that might insult some gods. Although the Abrahamic deities tend to not mind that. They're a bloodthirsty lot, honestly. And they also tend to ignore magicians or supplicants unless you pray every day for nine or eighteen days straight.

26

Pact to the Daemoness Astaroth.

This basic pact outline is a lot like any pact to any deity/daemon.

You ask Astaroth to assist you in working towards your goal, such as non-violent overthrown of a specific corporation, and you will do things for her in return.

Always set up the pact so that if she fails, you do not have to perform your end of the deal. Be fairly specific and make sure it's a desire you know you can accomplish. Don't ask for the impossible. No matter how many pacts I have made, I have yet to be included in ANY trip to the International Space Station. So keep it realistic.

And yes, I am aware of many people using magick and pacts to win at gambling.

But more are successful in launching new businesses or careers.

Or finding love and starting a family.

I assisted my daughter in a pact with a goddess to have a career with animals. It started with a job at a pet store, making contacts with people from an animal rescue, then working for that rescue. Then she wanted to be a Vet Tech, and that manifested within a year of being at the first rescue, and now she's the senior Vet Tech at a cat sanctuary. All within 4 years.

A suggested way to write your pact is below. It's a modified version I have used for the Grecian gods. Just worded to make the pact with Astaroth as a daemon. This is simply a suggestion. You should write this in your own words and go into detail want you expect and what you will give in return. It's typical to also give her praise in online groups and forums when the magick begins to work.

Pacts can be amended at most anytime. Simply rewrite the pact and then work another ritual.

A good practice with a pact is to work weekly offerings to the daemons or gods, something simple, but enough to know you appreciate their work on your behalf.

Be wary, because if you cannot provide the timely offerings and praise, she will stop your desire.

Write this out on paper with magick ink and wait until in the pact ritual before signing it. Astaroth, as a daemon, WILL expect a drop of blood as your signature at the bottom. So be ready for this.

Sample pact:

I, _____ in deepest respect and admiration, hereby call upon the Great Daemoness Astaroth and humbly offer up to her [what you are offering] in exchange for [what you want].

I affirm that a pact with you, Astaroth, is my most heartfelt desire. I now dedicate myself to [how you wish to change or live].

By signing below, I do dedicate myself to [what you wish to become or have happen]

Below I offer my signature and drop of blood on top of my signature.

With this blood offering, I now seal this pact.

Then draw Astaroth's simple sigil here.

I typically go into great detail about what I want and how I wish for it to happen. To put the pact into action, you will need to work a ritual to Astaroth and complete the pact.

With pacts, it's a good habit to weekly work a fast ritual to Astaroth, and give her a small or simple offering. Doesn't have to be a drop of blood, as wine will work as well for a weekly offering.

Pact Ritual

Prepare the pact itself. Do not sign it at this point. With a pact, you will need to place a drop of blood on your signature AND on Astaroth's daemonic sigil as offering.

Light the incense and candles.

Lights off.

Cast your circle and run the Banishing of the Pentagram if it is needed.

Settle yourself in and relax.

Breathe deeply and allow yourself to go into a slight trance state.

Meditate for a moment on the goal of the ritual, and read over the petition you plan to use.

Now, summon Astaroth, saying her common ENN three times.

Tasa Alora foren Ashtaroth

Tasa Alora foren Ashtaroth

Tasa Alora foren Ashtaroth

Astaroth, Daemon of Power

Astaroth, Daemon of Wealth

I ask that you join with me in my space

Be with me! Commune with me!

Astaroth, it is my deepest desire we enter into a pact!

Read your petition

Astaroth, I ask that you agree to this pact and that you will work with me to make this pact successful.

Now, sign the pact. Prick your finger and place a drop of blood over your signature.

Astaroth! With my signature and with my blood, I now seal this pact with you! May our efforts result in great success!

At this point, ready the blood sacrifice. Price a finger and drop an additional drop of blood onto her sigil.

And in gratitude for you agreeing to this pact, I now sacrifice my living essence to you!

Hold her sigil up and touch it to the flame of her candle, and say,

To you, I give over my essence, Astaroth.

As the sigil burns, drop it into the fireproof container and make sure it burns completely. Stir the ashes to make sure it's totally consumed. After the ritual, toss the ashes outside, allowing them to be spread with the wind.

There is considerable debate over whether we should burn the pacts once sealed, or hang onto them. I fall into the "Save The Pact" camp. After a few pacts, I have found it helps to refer back to a pact to make sure the spirit is doing their part!

Time to finish the ritual.

I thank you for being here with me, Astaroth, and you may now depart and please come again when I next call upon you!

27

Pact to the Goddess Astaroth

Like the pact to Astaroth as Daemoness, making a pact with the Goddess aspect is really straightforward and also the same as the pact to her as a Daemoness.

Big exceptions: *No blood offerings.* I suggest red wine, flowers, pure incense resins, and perhaps even baking sweet desserts for Astaroth, such as a cake or delicious bread. Heavy cream and honey is always a good choice as well.

Sample pact

I, _____ in deepest respect and admiration, hereby call upon the Goddess Astaroth and humbly offer up to her [what you are offering] in exchange for [what you want].

I affirm that a pact with you, Astaroth, is my most heartfelt desire. I now dedicate myself to [how you wish to change or live].

By signing below, I do dedicate myself to [what you wish to become or have happen]

And I hereby seal this pact.

Then draw Astaroth's simple sigil here.

I typically go into great detail about what I want and how I wish for it to happen. Wait until you are in the pact ritual before signing the pact. This means you will need the ink and a pen handy while working this ritual.

Ritual to Activate the Petition

For the pact ritual, you will just need her dedicated candles.

When ready, light the incense and candles. If you are using charcoal and resin, make sure to get that charcoal puck going. It should be covered in white ash before starting the ritual.

Drop some incense onto the glowing charcoal, and cast your circle. If you are using a temporary altar space, be sure to work the Banishment as well, to eject any non-beneficial energy from your space.

Here are the basic steps in an easy-to-follow list:

Light incense and candles

Cast your circle

Sit and meditate for a moment.

Now call to Astaroth

Astaroth! Goddess of Life, Goddess of the Field, Goddess of the Hearth.

Astaroth, you who have been known by name

names,

> *Astarte, Iananna, Venus, and others,*
> *Join with me in my space, talk with me,*
> *Grace me with your divine presence.*
> *Astaroth! I call to you now in your form as a* Loving Goddess.

Pause a moment - stretch out your awareness to see if she is near you now.

> *Astaroth, I wish to enter into a pact with you. Allow me to read this pact and I ask that you please agree to this.*

Read your pact out loud. After reading it, pause a moment to see how Astaroth reacts. Chances are, she has already agreed to the pact.

Pause now, and visualize the outcome of your pact manifesting. Run a daydream where it all occurs for you in the way you wish for it to manifest. Take your time doing this. (Hint: This is actually the key to how it all works.)

Now, sign the pact at the bottom as outlined above.

Pick up the offering and now say:

> *Oh Astaroth, please accept this humble offering, in gratitude for entering into a pact with you! I wish us great success!*

Place the offering into the offering bowl, and place that on her sigil.

Now, time to charge the petition or sigil with energy.

Hold your hands over the petition or sigil and say the following:

Intro this pact I now direct great power, power from you, Astaroth, and my own inner power, to make this desire manifest. And so it is!

After a minute or two, the pact is activated.

(There is some discussion about pacts at this point. Some say to burn the pact. Others say to hang onto it. I prefer to hang into it, to make sure the god or goddess is honoring their end of the bargain.

Oh, Goddess Astaroth, our time now is done. I thank you for your presence in my circle. You may depart peacefully now and please return when I next call upon you!

At this point, the initial ritual is completed.

28

Worksheets

As a bonus, I have created some worksheets to assist you in determining your desire, as well as some worksheets to help you create a Chaos sigil for this desire.

Each sheet is to be printed on US Letter Sized paper. But it should fit just fine on European sized letter paper as well.

Go here to access the downloads:

https://davepsychic.com/astaroth-downloads/

Desire Worksheet

This worksheet will guide you through the basic steps to define your desire in such a way as to write an effective petition. It's simple and pretty self-explanatory. Make as many copies as you need.

First, list your desire(s). Use a separate form for each desire type. Make a different list for each type of desire. One list for money. One for Love. And so on. Don't combine desires.

Second section is for WHY you want this desire. By stating

WHY, you can begin to formulate all the various WAYS this feeling evoked by the desire can happen. The feeling of LOVE, for example, can be a feeling of security, a feeling of family, a feeling of being wanted. But what else can evoke that feeling? By focusing on the feeling, you can determine ways to get that feeling NOW, which will bring you closer to manifesting that desire.

Next section is for listing the things you DO NOT want. Next to this column is WHY you do not want that item or desire.

Working this will allow you to determine what you need to do to shift your mindset so that the reasons listed in column two are false. As you work through each negative thought, you will begin to see that your desire is easily obtained, and that there is no reason to doubt that your desire will arrive.

Chaos Sigil Worksheet

After defining your desire, you can also turn it into a Chaos sigil. This worksheet will assist in this process, but it only outlines the basic sigil creation methods. For more advanced methods, look for my High Magick 101 Workbook and Ritual Log, available as a paperback on Amazon and Barnes & Noble.

This worksheet should only be filled out AFTER the Desire Worksheet is finished.

29

Astaroth Goddess Sigil

You could use a small statue of Inana, or perhaps Ishtar, and say it's Astaroth. You wouldn't be wrong.

However, I created this sigil for Astaroth which is tuned to her energy as a Goddess. It's already activated, so print it out (download it - see Appendix) as many times as you need. One is good for your altar, and perhaps have a talisman made from this design to carry with you.

Please, do not copy this design and make talismans for sale anywhere. Besides being an infringement of my copyright, the energy possessed by this sigil will stop working for you.

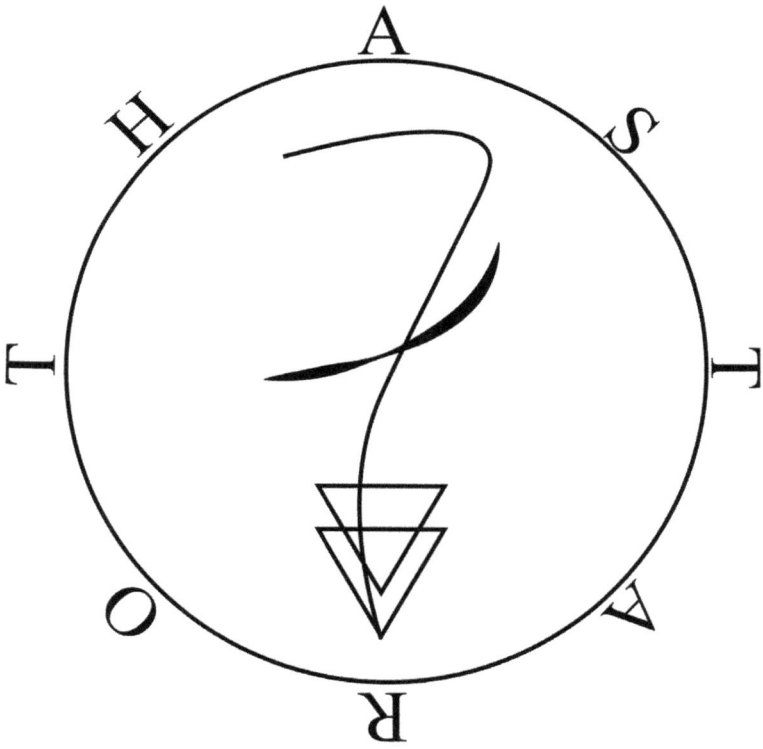

30

Astaroth's Daemon Sigil

I created this sigil while in contact with Astaroth.

This sigil is unlike any other and is tied to her energy as a daemon. Therefore, it's charged and tied to her energy and will work a lot better than the traditional sigils found on the internet or in existing texts.

The downloads (see appendix) have multiple sizes of this sigil for printing. Each page will give you a size to use on your altar, a size to use as blood offering, and a size to carry with you in a purse or wallet.

DAVID THOMPSON

Astaroth

31

Astaroth's Master Sigils

Power Draw Master Sigil

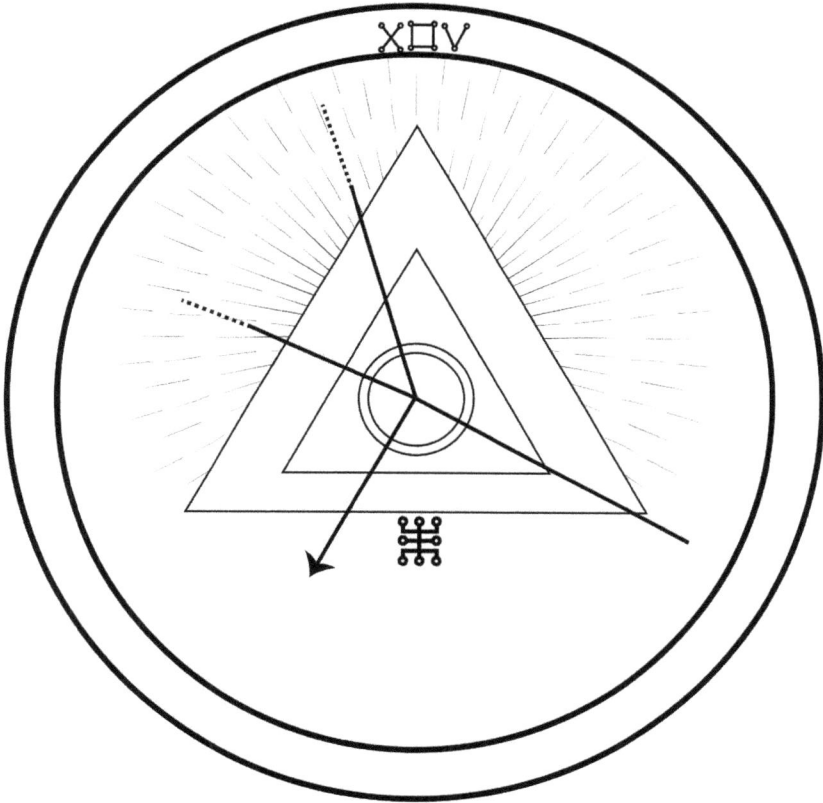

Wealth Draw Master Sigil

32

Magick Ink Recipe

If you don't purchase specific magick ink, buy some cheap fountain pen ink, or drawing ink in a bottle.

Find a small bottle with a good cap. Transfer some ink into the bottle (eyedropper works).

Prick a finger with a diabetic lancet, and let a few drops fall into the small bottle.

Cap, and shake to mix.

Now you have a bottle of Magick Ink.

If you wish, you can just drop the blood into the entire bottle of ink. Just don't use it for anything non-magick.

Black Salt Recipe

Collect some burned paper (not fully burned into gray ash, just blackened) or use a small piece of incense charcoal.

Crush the charcoal or grind up the burned paper in a mortar. Add a few spoonfuls of regular sale. Using the pestle, crush the salt together with the charcoal.

Now you have a supply of black salt.

Please note: *You can use ANY salt*. If it says "Salt" on the package, it's ok to use it here.

Another note: *This Black Salt is not like the black salt*

used in cooking. Do not use this black salt in cooking. Also, do not buy cooking black salt and think it'll have the same properties as magick black salt. Two different things.

Links

Sigils and Worksheets:
https://davepsychic.com/astaroth-downloads/
The Talimancer on Facebook:
https://www.facebook.com/thetalimancer1

33

Lesser Banishing of the Pentagram (Author's Revision)

Stand in the center of your room facing east.

Relax. Stand with arms at your side.

First thing reconnect to the universe.

Imagine growing larger and larger. Your point of view rises towards the ceiling in your space, and out above your house (unless you are outside)

Now, imagine you are raising above your neighborhood. Keep growing larger and larger.

You rise above the entire area, then keep growing and rise above the town. Then you are so high, you begin to see the entire earth. Keep rising up as you now speed past our Sun, and further out until all you see is the galaxy, its magnificent arms spreading out in every direction.

Keep growing and rising until above you appears a huge funnel, with streamers of colorful light flowing all around. Soak in this energy, allow the energy to fill you.

Breathing slowly, bring your self back to your space.

Close your eyes and raise your right hand above your head, pointing at the ceiling with a finger
Say:

"You are"

With your arm straight, swing your hand in front of you until you are pointing at the floor between your feet
Say:

"This Universe."

Still pointing at the floor, bend your elbow and bring your hand up until you are pointing at your right shoulder
Say;

"The Power"

Move your hand across your chest and point at your left shoulder
Say:

"And The Glory"

Bring both palms together to your chest (as if in prayer)
Say:

"Forever, So be it"

Return your left hand to the side and point directly in front of you with your right hand (like pointing at the rising sun or moon)
Make a small circle in front of you, clockwise and say:
"Tetra"
Now, move to face the south, and repeat the circle and say:
"Gram"
Again, move to face the west and make the small circle, saying;

"Mut"

Turn to the north, and repeat the circle motion, saying:

"Ton"

Turn so that you are facing east again.

Using the finger of your right hand, make a huge STAR in the air in front of you

Now say:

"I send from this place all intruding forces. They shall go far away and be powerless to interfere with my wishes, my thoughts, or my emotion. So be It"

34

Color Correspondences

Here are the meanings of different candle colors in general:

White candles-Destruction of negative energy, peace, truth and purity

Purple candles- Spiritual awareness, wisdom, tranquility

Lavender Candles– Intuition, Paranormal, Peace, Healing

Blue and Deep Blue Candles– Meditation, Healing, Forgiveness, Inspiration, Fidelity, Happiness, and opening lines of Communication.

Green Candles– Money, Fertility, Luck, Abundance, Health (not to be used when diagnosed with Cancer), Success

Rose and Pink Colored Candles– Positive self-love, friendship, harmony, joy

Yellow Candles- Realizing and manifesting thoughts, opening up communication, confidence, bringing plans into action, creativity, intelligence, mental clarity, clairvoyance.

Orange Candles– Joy, energy, education, strength attraction, stimulation

Red or Deep red Candles– Passion, energy, love, lust, relationships, sex, vitality, courage.

Black Candles– Protection, absorption and destruction of negative energy and also repelling negative energy from others

Silver candle– Goddess or feminine energy, remove negativity, psychic development, money

Gold candle– Male energy, Solar energy, fortune, spiritual attainment, money.

Candle colors and Days:

Sunday– Gold or yellow candles

Monday– Silver, Grey or White

Tuesday-Red

Wednesday-Purple

Thursday– Blue

Friday-Green

Saturday– Black or Purple

Days of the week:

Sunday = The day of the Sun. Useful for healing, creativity, success.

Monday = The day of the Moon (Hecate). Travel, fertility, farming, psychic powers.

Tuesday = The day of Mars (Ares). Overcoming challenges, cursing others, psychic attack.

Wednesday = The day of Mercury (Hermes). Magick that needs communication,

Thursday = The day of Jupiter (Zeus). Business, money, wealth, abundance.

Friday = The day of Venus (Aphrodite). Love and family rituals work best this day.

Saturday = The day of Saturn. Banishing, karma retribution, protection, curse breaking.

Moon Phases:

New Moon = Restarts. Work magick intended to bring to you anything.

New Moon to Full Moon (Waxing Moon) = Magick to start a business, garden, romance. Think of this period as the "Bring to me" phase.

Full Moon= Major magick time. Working with a moon goddess (Hecate) at this point in time. Energy builds as the moon grows full, and timing for this is anywhere from two days before the full moon to one day after full moon.

Full Moon towards New Moon (Waning Moon). Magick to release things. Magick to break curses, remove blocks, remove toxic people.

Helpful Links:

Planetary Hour Calculator:
  https://www.astrology.com.tr/planetary-hours.asp

Moon Phase Calculator:
  https://www.astrology.com.tr/moon-calendar.asp

ABOUT THE AUTHOR

Dave is an author of adult fantasy (The Furies series) as well as author of occult books about magick.

David began working ritual magick back in the 1970s. He took a brief break, then used the power of this magick to create a photography career which took him to Los Angeles and work as a photographer for multiple magazines.

David has studied magick in all forms, and in 2018, released a three-part magick instruction course in High Magick. Thousands of students have benefited from David's unique teaching style, making ceremonial magick accessible to everyone.

This book on Astaroth is book 7 in his High Magick Series.

Dave also has a series on Grecian Magick, exploring the aspects of ceremonial magick with the gods and goddesses of ancient Greece.

Dave's Facebook Page:

https://www.facebook.com/DavePsychic/

Secrets of Magick Facebook Group:

https://www.facebook.com/groups/secretsofmagick

Join the Grecian Magick Facebook group!
https://www.facebook.com/groups/grecianmagick

And finally, Dave's webpage, book readings and his services:
https://davepsychic.com

Sign-up for my Newsletter and get a FREE E-Book!
https://davepsychic.com/newsletter

www.ingramcontent.com/pod-product-compliance
Lightning Source LLC
Chambersburg PA
CBHW071932090426
42811CB00042B/2424/J